Cross-Training

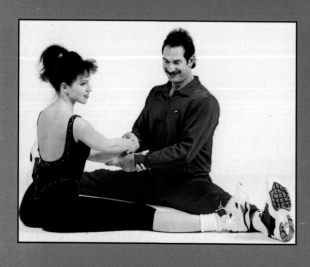

Tom Seabourne

Cross–Training

by

Tom Seabourne, Ph.D.

eddie bowers publishing, inc.
2600 Jackson Street
Dubuque, Iowa 52001-3342

Acknowledgments

Regards to my parents for their encouragement and my wife Danese for successfully completing her fourth pregnancy with a sense of humor.

Thanks to my mentors Zenryo Shimabuku, Soon Ho Chang, Vance McLaughlin, and the father of ultra–distance cycling John Marino.

To my four children, Alaina, Grant, Laura, and Susanna, who cross–train with me at the playground.

Ron Barker designed the cover and did all the photography. Deanna Irvin, Beth Means, Nicole Munsinger, and Hillary were the beautiful fitness models. David Freeman and Albert Funderburk drew the wonderful illustrations.

And a special thank you to Ernest Herndon, Miles Hall, and Eddie Bowers for editing and publishing Cross–Training.

eddie bowers publishing, inc.
2600 Jackson Street
Dubuque, Iowa 52001-3342

ISBN 0-945483-51-1

Contents

My definition of cross–training is:

A MENTAL–PHYSICAL–NUTRITIONAL–SPIRITUAL–SOCIAL–EMOTIONAL

APPROACH

USING SPECIALIZED

KNOWLEDGE AND TECHNIQUES

TO ACHIEVE PEAK PERFORMANCE

The purpose of cross–training is:

TO IMPROVE YOUR SPORT PERFORMANCE AND ENDURANCE

TO MAKE YOU FASTER, STRONGER, SMARTER, AND MORE

FLEXIBLE. TO MAKE YOU BETTER AT WHAT YOU DO.

Preface

More and more people are exercising less and less. Sixty–one percent of those who join a health club quit within the first four weeks. Many shirk responsibility concerning their health. It is easier to say "I don't have time" than to change exercise, stress management, and diet habits. Snake oil salesmen and researchers are teaming up in search of a magic bullet. Anti–oxidants, ginger, amino acids, vitamins and minerals, mushrooms, Coenzyme Q 10, garlic, soy extract, selenium, and shark cartilage are hoped to contain the secret shortcut to health and fitness.

Food–a–holics won't cut down until they want to. Fad diets don't work. Recently the government has chastised many of the leading weight–loss centers for false claims. Doctors sell different "programs." Scam diets include the latest "magical, miraculous, exotic, exclusive, new discovery breakthroughs." Many don't have a clue. Most have given up.

Infomercials display the latest fitness–fraud sauna wraps, rubber belts, vibrating machines, relaxacisers, and weighted belts. One infomercial disparages rubber–band resistance in favor of cheaper and more user–friendly models. Proponents of non–motorized treadmills say they are better than motorized, expensive ones. From newfangled rowers to step machines, Americans are eager to pay big bucks for a better body. The average Jane and Joe would rather pay $99.95 than stroll around the block three days a week.

There are more health clubs and low–fat foods than ever. Special pills may soon allow fat to pass through the body. Implants can change a skinny ectomorph into a muscular mesomorph. Do you see gym–rats whose bodies never change or obese people filling their grocery carts with low–fat cakes, cookies, and ice cream? Stomach stapling and gastric bypass surgery are on the rise. Fat–reducing creams are tempting, but where does the fat go? What happens when you stop using the cream? Why are Americans in worse shape than ever?

Cross–Training answers all these questions and more in a practical, simple, and personal method to help you trim down and tone up, lower blood pressure, look and feel good, energize yourself, ignite your immune system, decrease anxiety, head off health problems, increase your flexibility, delay aging, increase your independence, self–confidence, sense of achievement, and disease-proof your body. Cross–Training will teach you the secrets to exercise, diet, and stress management. You will learn to lift weights, stretch, eat correctly, and de–stress yourself without expensive diet programs or cumbersome equipment. Researchers at the Aerobics Center in Dallas state that "optimal health and quality of life are only achieved from appropriate fitness levels in aerobic fitness, flexibility, and endurance--a triad dubbed balanced fitness." Cross–Training takes the guesswork out of your fitness program with cartoons and personal anecdotes in a humorous easy–to–read format.

Be careful. I have never seen a training program or book I fully agree with. Parts of Cross–Training may not fit your lifestyle. Use what works for you and discard the rest.

Benefits of Cross-Training

I spend a lot of time on my bike listening to the radio. I heard a story about a man and his wife who were arguing. In a fit of rage the husband soaked the woman with gasoline and set her on fire. Neighbors managed to douse her and put out the fire. As soon as they left, he did it again.

According to *On An Average Day In America*, a car is stolen every thirty–three seconds, a robbery occurs every seventy–six seconds, a woman is raped every eight minutes, someone is shot every forty–three minutes, an individual is murdered every twenty–seven minutes, forty–thousand deaths each year are due to auto accidents, one–hundred–twenty–five–thousand deaths each year are from adverse reactions to prescription drugs, someone dies from heart disease every thirty–two seconds, and sixty million women, fifty million men, and ten million teenagers are over–fat. From where does this hurricane of anger and stress come from? In today's gripping societal vice, the question is not who struggles but who does not. The mark of success is being able to handle this yoke of pressure. For some, unfortunately, outlets include alcohol, drugs, and violence. Others race cars, jump out of airplanes, or shave their heads. One method of handling stress is neither illegal nor dangerous. It's called cross–training.

Cross–training is no panacea, but it can help. Bo Jackson knows what cross–training is. Cross–training combines various forms of exercise, healthy eating, and a positive attitude to build body and mind from the inside out. It is not related to cross–dressing. Cross–training diffuses aggression and increases socialization. Most are well aware of the benefits of cross–training; they just have no intention of getting off the couch. A survey of over one–thousand inactive people who said they wanted to exercise but didn't have the time found that eighty–four percent watched an average of three hours of TV daily. Dr. Dishman concluded that people who use time as an excuse are no busier than cross–trainers. They choose not to make time to work out. Dr. Kevin Patrick of the United States Department of Health and Human Services reported that sedentary living greatly increases the chances of obesity, heart attack, stroke, cancer, and bone demineralization. Beginning cross–trainers are surprised at how much better they feel doing chores and activities they enjoy. Gardening burns 300 calories per hour! Paradoxically, the less conditioned they are, the more they benefit from even the simplest activities. Dr. Rod Dishman's research demonstrated that people who exercised enjoyed enhanced self–image and health, psychological benefits, and a feeling of achievement.

Cross–training improves cardiovascular endurance, flexibility, muscular endurance, muscular strength, body composition, concentration, and coordination. You can be male or female, nine to ninety. Cross–trainers choose activities they enjoy. They make eating and exercise commitments and feel empowered by their choices. They turn each training session into a positive experience. They forget about hard–to–please coaches. Adults generally don't have much fun; cross–training adults do. They pick sports that fit their lifestyle. Play isn't what you do; it's how you feel about what you do. Cross–trainers walk, roller–blade, or ride bikes. They take multi-vitamins, laugh a lot, sleep well, and choose programs that give them a lift. According to the November, 1994 issue of *Muscle & Fitness*, the most popular cross–training activities include fitness walking, swimming, cycling, bowling, basketball, billiards, and aerobics. And there are hundreds of others from table tennis to bocce! Simply combine your favorite activities and you are a cross–trainer:

Cross-Training Activities

Upper body (e.g. rowing, swimming),

Lower body (e.g. in–line skating, stair climbing),

Strength (e.g. weight training, calisthenics),

Endurance (e.g. fitness walking, jumping rope),

Rhythmic (e.g. bicycling, hiking),

Skill (e.g. racket sports, basketball),

Pounding movements (e.g. jogging, aerobic dance)

Gliding (e.g. sliding, stairmaster).

Cross–training is fun. Psychologist Dr. William Menninger explained that good mental health depends on a person's ability to play. An individual should budget some time for play and take it seriously. Mental health is directly related to physical health. Have you ever been really sick? Cross–trainers don't take their health for granted. They awake at dawn and give thanks for a new day of cross–training. Cross–training increases self–esteem, energy, creativity, sociability, and productivity.

Cross–training makes you smarter. Alan Hartley, Ph.D., from Scripps College in Claremont, California, studied three hundred adults aged fifty–five to eighty–eight years old. Those who cross–trained had better memories, reasoning abilities, and problem–solving skills. Dennis Lobstein, Ph.D., a wellness director at New Mexico Highlands University, claimed that eighty percent of the population suffers from exercise deficiency syndrome. When we don't exercise, we get stressed out. We get sick and depressed. If we exercise, chemicals are released in our brain that make us feel better.

Cross–training prevents injuries, alleviates boredom, and curbs burn–out. Stress injuries are among the most common problems seen by primary care physicians who treat active individuals. The weekend warrior suffers with tennis elbow or a marathoner tiptoes in with painful shins. Hardcore runners pound the pavement, sometimes grimacing, sometimes limping. If a cross–trainer notices she is developing a running injury, she switches to biking. They use good judgment and listen to what their bodies tell them.

Strength training is an area we neglect as we grow older, but there is a greater need for it as we age, maintains William Evans, Ph.D., director of physiology at Penn State University. Cross–weight trainers don't max out every workout. They cycle their programs so their minds and bodies lift to improve their performance in other sports, but they don't neglect the demands of their particular specialty. Bicycling cross–trainers don't grow so muscular that they struggle uphill carrying an extra load of cosmetic beef. Cross–training is a balanced approach to fitness. Unlike a professional tennis player's Popeye–like forearm or a computer wizard's overused left brain, cross–training is a complete mind–body conditioner. Most sports require a combination of strength, endurance, skill, and concentration. The best athletes achieve fitness with a variety of activities and techniques. Cross–training may offer beginners, intermediates, and champions a step up toward their illusive perfect game.

Cross–trainers know the importance of mental conditioning. They use physical training as a tool to gain self–knowledge and are never so stubborn, so successful, so confident that they are not constantly seeking a mental edge. A focused athlete is a better athlete. Cross–training enhances thought processes to develop a total package. Cross–sport trainers use their competitors to make them better. Some use spirituality to keep them balanced.

Cross–training allows a person to become who they were meant to be. They trade a wasted afternoon of TV, chips, and beer for a productive hour of exercise, fruit, and a turkey sandwich. Or, cross–trainers quit smoking and go for a walk. Cross–training does not have to be grunting and sweating. The action can be as simple as raking leaves and walking the dog. A walk around the block can be combined with climbing a flight of stairs. Break your cross–training into mini-sessions performed throughout the day. A life of balance, moderation, and simplicity is a cross-trainer's signature. Training the body in this manner disciplines the mind to stop expecting something for nothing.

For twenty–five years the American Heart Association identified smoking, high blood pressure, and high cholesterol as the risk factors for heart disease. In 1994, they added "not exercising." Dean Ornish, M.D., assistant clinical professor of medicine at the University of California, San Francisco, presented data demonstrating that a low–fat diet, stress management, and exercise form a non–surgical, cross–training approach to combatting heart disease, high blood pressure, and diabetes. Not only can your health be strengthened but so can your bank account. According to Ornish, it's easier to get a person to eat low–fat, exercise, and do stress management than to diet and exercise sporadically. His results showed that people who submerged themselves into an eating, exercise, and stress management program realized significant short term results, motivating them to continue for the long haul.

Watch cross–trainers. Surrounded by noise, they glide to their music. A cyclist can grab a twenty dollar bill blowing down the road. A walker can feel a cool breeze. A runner notices a patrol car hiding around the bend. It's easier to nudge the gas pedal than to race–walk up a hill, but the driver does not see the doe hiding behind a tree. Nature invites cross–trainers into her private scenes.

Workouts push cross–trainers to higher levels of endurance, but they understand the misconception "no pain, no gain." Their minds switch from left to right, tuning into a relaxed focus. Cross–training is pure freedom. Bodies play, recover, and play again. Cross–trainers work hard, enjoy their play, and smile often. They are simply waiting for the next miracle. Cross–training is not just sport, it's life.

FITNESS

Just Do It, Right

Did your pudgy, cigar–smoking physical education teacher force you to run? Were you required to "drop for ten" after each lap? Running and push–ups is cross–training. Your P.E. teacher taught you to hate cross–training. Seventy-four percent of students said they had negative experiences in high school physical education classes. If you "just did it," you did it wrong. Ease into your cross–training program. Progress gradually.

Rules and Regulations
(Items 1 - 23)

1. Your cross-training routine should be easy. If you don't love it you won't do it.

2. Weights work! Train each body part twice a week.

3. It's O.K. to do aerobics every day. You may vary the activity.

4. If playing tennis bothers your ankles, ride a bike. If riding a bike hurts your knees, try the Stairmaster.

5. Both under-eating and under-sleeping can hurt your cross-training.

6. Avoid cross-training with your significant other, unless one of you promises not to act like a big shot.

7. Incorporate stretching into cross-training.

continued

8. Alternate hard and easy days if you cross-train using similar activities such as basketball and tennis.

9. Cross-train to gain without the pain.

10. Pre-schedule meals in advance.

11. Become sensitive to cross-training energy needs.

12. No skipping meals.

13. Eat two servings of carbohydrates and one serving of protein at each meal.

14. Remember cross-eating and cross-training speed up the metabolism.

15. Consume most of your calories early in the day.

16. Cross-train before work to make sure you get it in.

17. For a change of pace, occasionally cross-train with a partner.

18. Develop an indoor cross-training program in case of inclement weather.

19. Strategize a cross-training routine when you travel.

20. If you're short on time, cross-train in small increments throughout the day.

21. Regular endurance exercise without strength training does not prevent muscle loss.

22. When you are at home eat the right kind of foods.

23. Treat yourself to a "forbidden food" once a week.

Been There Done That

Kinesiologists claim that simply playing different sports is cross–training. When I was young, I cross–trained all summer. I cycled ten miles to the tennis courts and hit balls all morning. After a sack lunch, I sparred with a karate buddy and rode home. In your youth I bet you cross–trained too. Are you cross–training now? Have you grown an inner–tube around your waist to cross–train at the beach? Grab the skin under your chin. Do you resemble a cross–training turkey?

Activities That Can
Work For You

Pump Iron

Count the years since you cross–trained. Let's start smart! Combine resistance training with aerobics. Aerobics does not replace strength work. Wanna–be bodybuilders sweat bullets on the stairmaster, exercise bicycle, and versa–climber rather than doing squats, lunges, and deadlifts. That's like consuming a half–gallon of ice–cream in hopes of adding size to your pectorals and triceps. Save aerobics for fat–burning, and pump iron to shape and tone your muscles.

Aerobic Golf

Aerobics isn't sprinting on planet Reebok or paying mega–bucks for a cross country ski–machine/coat rack. Find a passion. Save the cart–fee and golf becomes aerobic. Walk briskly between holes. Pay a caddie to get some exercise lugging your bag. Walking the course gives professional golfers time to plan strategy for their next shot. Gerald Fletcher, M.D., wrote that golf improves agility, mental acuity, focus, and friendships. If you add relaxation, fresh air, and walking, the health benefits can be enormous. An average nine–hole course is two miles, and eighteen holes is a four–mile workout. A new fad is speed–golf. Competitors run between shots, and their score is determined by combining strokes and time.

Cardiovascular Racket Sports

Racket sports are aerobic if you speed–walk to gather balls between points. Smash balls to your opponent while he runs you ragged stroking cross–court and down the line. Never stop moving. Hit serves on the run. While waiting to return serve, bounce around. Your opponent is your personal trainer.

Endurance Basketball

A basketball pick–up game is aerobic–plyometrics if you shuffle and shadow–box between power jams. Your feet never stop. Get open or cover a man. Take a jam–box to the court. Music livens up the game. Get started and keep going. Dr. Mihalyi Csikszentmihalyi, University of Chicago researcher and author of *Flow: The Psychology of Optimal Experience*, said it takes about 20 minutes to get things moving on their own. He calls this period following the warmup "activation energy." Others describe it as steady–state or momentum.

In-Line Skating

Every Saturday I do aerobic baby–sitting. I take my children for a roller–blade stroller ride to the playground. My kids enjoy roller–coaster speeds while I clutch the stroller for dear life. In–line skating develops lower body strength and cardiovascular fitness. To maintain a high intensity, use a constant rhythmic pattern with your arms and legs, minimizing glide. Develop a side–to–side movement. Swing your arms for balance and speed.

Step-Ups

Upon arriving at the playground, I pull my running shoes from the stroller and we practice step–ups on the miniature balance beam. You can do step–ups on almost any piece of playground apparatus. Try step–ups on a four inch bench. Watch your feet as you put your right foot up, then your left foot up, then your right foot down, and your left foot down. Keep your feet close to your bench. Place your entire foot on the bench. Step off on the ball of your foot and then roll to your heel. Continue for fifteen minutes. Progress gradually to prevent injury.

Stair Climbing

An even safer method of step–ups is the stair climbing machine. Researchers at California State University, Northridge, found that runners and stair climbers improved their maximum oxygen consumption equally; but the runners had injuries and dropouts while the stair climbers had no injuries or dropouts. Stair climbing is considered low impact because the feet never leave the machine. There is no strain on ligaments or joints, and the intensity is monitored and controlled by you. Researchers at the University of Massachusetts in Amherst studied twenty college students and discovered that running burned an average of fifteen calories per minute, in–line skating burned fourteen calories, and stair climbing burned eleven calories per minute.

Rowing

If you don't have access to a canoe, indoor rowing is a low impact, total body workout. It works your hips, abdominals, arms, trunk, legs, and shoulders. Rowing can help tone muscles as well as improve your cardiovascular system. I have my rowing machine in front of the television because it is the most boring indoor exercise in existence.

Sliding

Sliding, or lateral training, is a new fitness fad. You slip booties over your shoes and move side to side on a slideboard. Sliding burns twice as many calories as treadmill training, according to Robert Otto, Ph.D., director of the Human Performance Laboratory at Adelphi University. He claims the extra resistance is similar to walking while dragging your feet.

Fitness Walking

Aerobics in the 1990's is fitness–walking. Researchers at Brown University found that the government could save money on down–time and health care if they paid people to walk. Walking is easy on your body. You have seen them, pumping up and down hills like toy soldiers. They are conversing in groups, or they are alone: robo–walking, dedicated, focused. CNN addicts aerobicize on their treadmills. According to *Men's Fitness* magazine, beginning treadmillers should walk at a comfortable pace for three to five minutes, then walk fifteen minutes at a faster pace by taking longer strides, followed by a five minute cool–down. Advanced treadmill trainers should warm up, repeat the second phase of the workout, and then raise the angle of incline to ten percent for fifteen minutes, with a five minute cool–down.

Walk This Way

Stand with your feet together and lean forward from the ankles. Wherever your foot falls determines your proper stride length. Take another stride and keep your supporting leg straight as your body passes over it. Try to keep your rear foot on the ground as long as possible before pushing off. Roll from the heel of your foot, through the arch, and onto the ball before "toeing off." Bend your elbows at ninety degrees and swing your arms back–and–forth just below chest level, without crossing the midline of your body. Lean forward from the ankles instead of the waist. Stand tall and keep your head up with your eyes focused several feet ahead. Relax your shoulders and hands, but keep your stomach in and your chin parallel to the ground. Stay loose.

Do It Your Way

You don't need me to teach you how to walk. Fitness gurus will take your money to teach you how they walk. Walk naturally, smooth and steady. Walk in the morning before breakfast or in the evening after dinner, once or twice a day. Two miles in thirty minutes will strengthen your heart without sacrificing hard–

earned muscle. Start slow. Speed up if the mood strikes. The average woman's daily activity involves walking ten miles, and the average man walks seven miles.

Striding Hills

Walk hills for variation. In 1994, the Cooper Clinic in Dallas conducted a study determining whether walking at a fast pace was harder than walking slower on an incline. Results demonstrated that walking slower on an incline was perceived easier but burned more calories than walking faster. Be careful on the downhill. Walking downhill forces your muscles to contract eccentrically. Eccentric contractions cause delayed onset muscle soreness (DOMS). Research suggests that DOMS is partly responsible for the high dropout rate of eager exercisers.

Backpacking and Hiking

Backpacking is a terrific way to stay on your exercise program while on vacation. An eight–hour hike over uneven terrain burns as many calories as a twenty–mile walk, not to mention the caloric expenditure of carrying a forty-pound pack. Backpacking is a natural stress management strategy – if you remember to take a compass.

Cross–Country Skiing

Cross–country skiing exercises both the lower and upper body. Research demonstrates that cross–country skiers are the most aerobically fit individuals on the planet. More calories are burned during cross–country skiing than during other aerobic activities. The large amount of muscle mass involved makes cross–country skiing intense, but it places little pressure on joints. There is even less pressure on joints when your indoor cross–country ski machine doubles as a coat rack.

Swimming

Back problems or knee pain may prevent you from walking or jogging. A non–impact, aerobic answer to your dilemma is swimming. Swimming laps burns about twenty–five percent more calories than running in a given time period. However, swimming in cold water may increase fat stores under the skin. My fat stores double after cold water swimming because my appetite quadruples.

Aqua–Running

The aquatic medium supports the body, taking pressure off joints and bones in the back and legs. Aqua–running is excellent for overweight individuals or those with arthritis. Running in water dissipates heat more readily so there is less perceived effort. Run in water waist to chest deep. Push off the bottom with your feet. To raise your intensity, run faster or lift your knees higher. The land-running movements are exaggerated by pumping the arms and legs through a full range of motion. It's easy to slow down and inadvertently slack off, so try and keep the same pace as you do on dry land. Florida State University researchers monitored aqua–runners and treadmill runners and found that there were no significant differences in maximum aerobic capacity, anaerobic threshold, or running efficiency after six weeks of training. The researchers concluded that water running is an effective substitute to land running for the maintenance of cardiovascular fitness. In addition, running in water is beneficial to those who are rehabilitating an injury.

Cross–Training Shoes

Years ago when you felt a hole in your canvas tennis shoes (with gum rubber soles) you bought a new pair for four dollars. Contemporary athletic shoes are more comfortable, durable, complicated, and expensive. Invest in a good pair of walking or jogging shoes depending on your foot type. If you are big (you know who you are), be sure your shoes have thick heels to absorb impact. Your heel should be hugged by the shoe. The heel counter that fits around the outside of the heel should be firm. Bend them at the ball of the foot to test their flexibility. Walking shoes have a slightly lower heel and a stiffer heel counter than jogging shoes.

Foot Type

Determine your foot type and let your salesperson help you to choose the right shoe. Your decision should be based on how much you train, what surface you train on, and what foot problems you may have. A pronated foot leans inward with each step. The inside of the foot touches the ground first and the foot appears to roll outward. A cross–trainer with neutral feet finds his toes and heel are aligned with the ground and lower leg. A supinated foot tilts outward with each step. The outer side of the foot touches the ground first and the foot rolls inward. Examine your shoes for wear and decide whether you are a pronator, supinator, or vegitator.

Purchasing Shoes

Measure both feet properly to fit your shoes. Your feet swell as the day progresses, so purchase your shoes later in the day. Wear the same type of socks you use for your cross–training. New shoes don't have to be broken–in. They should feel good immediately. After six months or three hundred miles, check the outer sole for wear. More than five hundred miles and your midsoles are shot. If duct tape is the primary forefoot cushion, it's time to rob your piggy bank. Name brands can wear out as fast as generics.

Breathing

Riding a bike, walking, and running require deep breathing. Breathing in ozone, carbon monoxide, sulphur dioxide, nitrogen dioxide, and lead can impede your performance and cause wheezing, coughing, headaches, and nausea. Untreated, these pollutants can lead to bronchitis, emphysema, and pneumonia.

To Avoid Pollution:

1. Cross–train before or after rush hour.

2. Cross–train in windy areas around green grass and oxygen producing trees, away from car exhaust.

3. Check your newspaper for the Pollutant Standard Index. If it is high, train indoors.

4. If you feel uncommon fatigue, a tightness in your chest, or nausea, call it quits early.

5. Take anti–oxidants including vitamins C, E, and beta–carotene. These vitamins may protect cells from ozone contamination.

(To decide on your cross-training goals see Chart A on page 9.)

GOALS

Please circle the goals you would like to attain in your cross-training program

Lose some of my body fat	Quit smoking
Lower my cholesterol	Tone–up my muscles
Speed up my metabolism	Improve my sport performance
Eat right	Improve my cardiovascular endurance
Have more energy	Decrease my blood pressure
Prevent having a heart attack	Start a walking program
Prevent a stroke	Start a weight lifting program
Gain muscle	Improve my flexibility
Stay alert during the mid–afternoon	Handle stress
Prevent cancer	Live longer
Stop craving sugar	Learn to relax

2

EATING

Thin Is In

Cross–training will keep you halfway fit. The other half is eating. Despite low–fat foods and diet programs, Americans are fatter than ever. In the 1990's we gained an average of eight pounds according to the July 1994 edition of the *Journal of the American Medical Association*. In 1994, American dieters spent thirty–two billion dollars trying to get thin.

Eat Frequently

What if I said you could go off your diet, lose your rumbling stomach, be less irritable, consume six meals a day, and actually lose body fat and feel great? You'd think it was another scam–diet claim. Six meals a day is a lifestyle change providing increased energy. If you took a month's worth of food on vacation, you wouldn't eat it all the first week. Likewise, rather than consuming three large meals, spread your calories into six small meals each day. Moving from three to six meals a day also helps lower your Low Density Lipoprotein (LDL) cholesterol according to McGrath and Gibney in the 1994 *European Journal of Clinical Nutrition*. Excess LDL cholesterol sticks to artery walls, blocking blood flow to the heart.

Cravings

Another study showed that eating six meals a day lowers insulin levels, decreasing cravings and subsequent binges. After three weeks of eating six quality meals a day, greasy foods and rich desserts are no longer to die for. You will desire what your body needs, not what some television commercial fools you into believing. My meals include a combination of protein such as chicken breasts, turkey breasts, fish, yogurt, cottage cheese, egg whites, or lean red meat with carbohydrates including fruits, vegetables, cereals, grains, or breads.

Diets Deprive Muscle

"Stop the insanity!" says a high–profile fitness guru. When you diet, you lose muscle, water, and fat. If you cut your calories to less than nine–hundred per day, for every ten pounds you lose, four of those pounds will be muscle. Each time you go on a diet, your body finds it easier to conserve fat. Skipping calories usually means skipping breakfast. If you miss breakfast, your body will fall into a starvation mode holding onto fat. When you finally eat, you may eat too fast or too much, causing an increase in insulin, resulting in increased fat storage.

Eat Later, Get Fatter

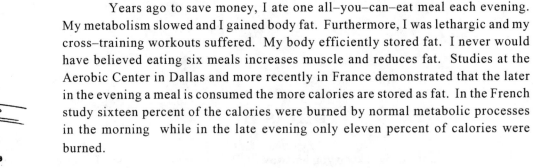

Years ago to save money, I ate one all–you–can–eat meal each evening. My metabolism slowed and I gained body fat. Furthermore, I was lethargic and my cross–training workouts suffered. My body efficiently stored fat. I never would have believed eating six meals increases muscle and reduces fat. Studies at the Aerobic Center in Dallas and more recently in France demonstrated that the later in the evening a meal is consumed the more calories are stored as fat. In the French study sixteen percent of the calories were burned by normal metabolic processes in the morning while in the late evening only eleven percent of calories were burned.

Fat

Dietary fat is the most concentrated source of energy, providing nine calories per gram compared with four calories per gram from either carbohydrates or protein. But fat is not the enemy. Essential fatty acids are required for maintenance of healthy skin and the regulation of cholesterol and hormones. Dietary fat allows many vitamins to be readily absorbed.

America's Top Ten Fat Sources	
1. Margarine	6. Ground beef
2. Whole milk	7. Low–fat milk
3. Shortening	8. Eggs
4. Mayonnaise and salad dressing	9. Butter
5. American cheese	10. Vanilla ice cream

According to a 1995 USDA survey

Excess Fat Is Stored

The dark side to fat is that the average American consumes a whopping sixty–three pounds per year. Excess fat sits on your body in globs. It is like a huge, billowy storage compartment. Muscle needs calories to move and grow. Muscles prefer to burn carbohydrates for energy and utilize protein for growth and repair. Consuming starchy carbohydrates increases your metabolic furnace. Too much fat is simply stored.

Good Fats

We need to consume some fat. But don't pig out on cake and ice cream. Some people balance their low–fat food with high fat. How many times have you seen someone eating a candy bar with a diet soft drink? There are different kinds of fat. A teaspoon of lard has approximately the same amount of calories as a teaspoon of olive oil. But olive, peanut, and canola oils are mono–unsaturated fats. These essential fatty acids (EFA's) have a cholesterol lowering effect, as long as your overall fat consumption is low. Other EFA's include safflower, corn, cottonseed, and soybean oils. Nuts, fish, and most seeds also contain significant amounts of EFA's. Fat that is hard at room temperature such as lard, cheese, dairy, and meat fat is saturated. Saturated fat tends to stick to blood vessel walls and raise cholesterol levels. Unsaturated fat such as oils are generally liquid at room temperature. At first fat enhances palatability, and most people would choose a calorically equivalent slice of apple pie rather than an apple. After three weeks of low–fat eating, your "fat tooth" may disappear.

Fat Replacements

Ten years ago it was difficult to eat low–fat. Now there is fat–free everything. According to the Food Marketing Institute, fat is the leading preoccupation of grocery shoppers. In 1994, a Calorie Control Counter survey revealed ninety percent of adult Americans chose fat–free products compared to seventy–six percent in 1991. Buyer beware. Low–fat is not always low–calorie. When fat disappears, sugar is likely to increase. If it is fat–free but the first three ingredients are sugar, corn syrup, and fructose, you are about to bite into a significant number of calories. Consuming large quantities of simple sugar raises your insulin, causing whatever calories you don't use for energy to be stored as fat. The good news is that breakfast time has changed for many Americans in the last ten years. Eggs, bacon, and breakfast meats have been replaced by bagels, muffins, and waffles according to the NPD Group, a market research company in Port Washington, New York.

Read the Label

1. **"Cholesterol–free"** means the cholesterol has been removed from the product.

2. **"Light"** means that the product has either half the fat, half the sodium, or two–thirds the calories of the regular version.

3. **"Low–fat"** means that the product gets no more than thirty percent of its calories from fat.

4. **"Reduced fat"** means that the product has to have at least twenty-five percent less fat than the regular product.

5. **"Fat–free"** means that the product has less than half a gram of fat per serving.

The Choice Is Yours

Many of us are addicted to high fat, high sugar foods that have little nutritional value but taste great. Baked chicken, tuna, brown rice, and egg whites may not compare to ice cream, hot dogs, and cotton candy; but tastes can be modified and habits altered. Students were allowed to choose from a variety of fruits, vegetables, meats, cakes, and ice cream. At first most chose desserts, but within two weeks they craved fruits and vegetables. Sooner or later, your body lets you know what it needs. If nutritious foods were as delicious as fat–filled meats and desserts, healthy eating would simply be a matter of choice. A study reported in the May, 1994 issue of the *American Journal of Clinical Nutrition* showed that subjects who ate less fat and more carbohydrates were happier and kept the weight off more effectively than those who simply counted total calories. Meena Shah, Ph.D., says for long term weight control, cut the fat.

Easy Fat Free Replacements

1. Saute in defatted chicken broth instead of oil.

2. A quarter cup of applesauce instead of a like amount of oil in muffin, cake, or cookie recipes.

3. Skim milk instead of whole milk.

4. Use powdered butter instead of butter.

5. Fat–free imitation sour cream instead of regular sour cream.

6. Evaporated skim milk instead of butter.

7. Corn syrup instead of oil in cookie recipes.

8. Yolk free egg noodles instead of regular pasta.

9. Angel food cake instead of high-fat desserts.

10. Non–fat plain yogurt instead of oil.

11. Non–stick skillet instead of a regular pan.

12. Two egg whites instead of one whole egg.

13. Replace regular cheese with fat–free cheese.

14. Pancakes instead of bacon and eggs.

15. Oven fried potatoes instead of french fries.

16. Chicken noodle soup instead of cream of chicken soup.

17. Pretzels instead of potato chips.

18. Salsa instead of bean dip.

19. Steamed vegetables instead of sauteed vegetables.

Meals

Each day I consume six small meals that I call mini-meals. Initially it was difficult getting in meals between breakfast and lunch, and between lunch and dinner. Now a mere five minutes is required to ingest pre–cut vegetables and chicken or non–fat yogurt while my colleagues are wolfing down soft drinks and chips. A recent investigation reported in the *New England Journal Of Medicine* revealed the need to eat several meals each day rather than just two or three. Those who grazed on seventeen meals found that their food was absorbed more efficiently and the nutrients were utilized more **effectively.** (Seventeen! I'm only suggesting you eat six). In addition their metabolic rates increased, and they lost body fat. Another study suggests we should eat a variety of different protein–amino acid combinations, complex carbohydrates, and a small amount of mono–unsaturated and unsaturated fats. It is also important to vary the number of calories you eat on a daily basis so your body doesn't adapt and lower its metabolism. Be creative. Cross–train the foods you eat.

Pre–Prepare Meals

Preparing meals is my Thursday night ritual. Cracking several dozen eggs and filling up five plastic containers with micro–waved egg whites, oatmeal, and raisins is relaxing. I carry one oatmeal, egg white, raisin container, along with tuna, MET–Rx, and a variety of fruits and vegetables to work each day, supplying breakfast through mid–afternoon meals. Preparing my meals in advance ensures that I won't be tempted to make a detour into a fast food establishment.

Eat for Energy

Eating frequently is an effective plan for any cross–trainer. Consume three meals and three mini–meals each day, and add extra carbohydrates to your post–workout meals. Your body can store twice as many grams of carbohydrates twice as fast if you consume them within thirty minutes of your workout. This window of opportunity is the best time to refuel muscle and liver glycogen stores. But it is not just energy. Your muscles need fuel for growth and repair. Your muscles get weaker when they run out of carbohydrates leading to possible injury says registered dietician Becky Zimmerman.

Eat to Fuel Your Workout

When you increase the frequency, intensity, or duration of your cross–training, add calories to each meal. Skimping on meals can weaken your immune system. Nutritional immunologist Tim Kramer suggests that if you exercise harder, you should increase your calories. In my first ultra–distance cycling race I did not eat enough and ended up losing ten pounds of muscle. It took me six months of eating and weight training to regain those precious myofibrils. To do this, I ate a complete meal every two hours. Each meal consisted of a serving of protein and two carbohydrates. I consumed whole foods such as oatmeal, brown rice, egg whites, cereal, vegetables, fruits, chicken, lean red meat, and fish. I never missed a feeding. The following year I rode my bike across America. I was in the saddle twenty–two hours a day for ten days. I rode over three hundred miles each day and didn't lose a pound of muscle. Part of the secret was that I consumed four hundred quality protein and carbohydrate calories every forty–five minutes!

Eat Smaller Meals

For fifteen years bodybuilders have known the secret for losing fat without sacrificing muscle. Six small, quick meals each day replace three marathon gorging sessions. Each meal includes a serving of protein and two servings of a carbohydrate. The following list consists of six meals a cross-trainer on a strict program might eat in a day.

Menu

1. **Breakfast:** An egg white omelet, oatmeal, and toast.

2. **Mini–meal:** Yogurt and a bagel.

3. **Lunch:** Tuna sandwich with fruit and vegetables.

4. **Mini–meal:** Rice cakes, non–fat cheese, carrots, and celery.

5. **Dinner:** Baked chicken, baked potato, and green beans.

6. **Mini–meal:** Fiber cereal, protein shake.

Individualized Program

Eating to energize workouts is tantamount to cross–training success. Cross–trainers individualize their diets to their workouts, but basic eating truths apply for all cross–trainers. Cross–trainers steer clear of fat and sugar and develop a taste for lean proteins, fibrous vegetables, and starchy carbohydrates. They develop an ongoing trial and error eating plan for peak performance. Karate star Ernie Reyes Jr. sometimes eats thirty egg whites a day. Professional bodybuilder Paul DeMayo may drink six MET–Rx protein shakes to feed his muscle. Some Dallas Cowboys were recently cited as junk food junkies until they started eating to fuel their workouts. Research suggests endurance athletes require significantly more protein than other athletes; therefore, weight training aerobicizers may find it beneficial to increase their intake of both protein and carbohydrates.

Treats

For months I ate the same non–fat, low–sugar diet. If a cake found its way into my house, I surreptitiously cut thin bite–sized pieces until the entire cake vanished. A half gallon of ice cream would magically disappear from the carton, one shovel full at a time. Now I occasionally allow myself a treat, and my body–fat is lower than when I pretended to be strict. Nutritionist Keith Klein recommends that if you sneak a piece of cake, don't blow it by consuming the whole cake. If you have a flat tire, would you slash the remaining three tires? Keith advises us to make better bad choices. Instead of chowing down on a carton of ice cream, savor a serving of non–fat frozen yogurt. Rather than blowing it on a pepperoni pizza, create a cheeseless vegetable pizza.

---

1. **Wendy's** Baked Potato: 270 calories, less than one gram of fat.

2. **Arby's** Light Roast Turkey Deluxe: 249 calories, 4 fat grams.

3. **Jack In The Box** Chicken Fajita Pita: 292 calories, 3 fat grams.

4. **Hardee's** Grilled Chicken Sandwich: 310 calories, 3 fat grams.

5. **McDonald's** Apple Bran Muffin: 180 calories, less than 1 fat gram.

6. **Long John Silver's** Baked Fish: 300 calories, 6 fat grams.

7. **Hardee's** Pancakes: 280 calories, less than 1 fat gram.

8. **Dunkin Donuts** Cinnamon 'N' Raisin Bagel: 250 calories, 2 fat grams.

9. **Taco Bell** Soft Chicken Taco: 213 calories, 4 fat grams.

10. **KFC** Mashed Potatoes: 35 calories, 1 fat gram.

11. **Subway** Six Inch Turkey Sandwich: 322 calories, 2 fat grams.

Condiments

Use seasoned vinegars, balsamic, or wine vinegars to season both salads and vegetables. Ground oatmeal can bread meats that you previously fried. Flour, ketchup, mustard, non-fat mayonnaise, non-fat salad dressing, and imitation butter flavor are other fat-saving alternatives.

Snacks

If you miss a meal, have a snack; but look out for clever advertisements. An energy bar claims to contain "delicious whole grain, no preservatives, and filling with real fruit." In reality the bar has more white flour than whole grain oats and more sugar than fruit. Another bar has a label saying "enriched granola" which really means sugar, almonds, crisp rice, and corn flakes. David Allison, associate research scientist at the Obesity Research Center of St. Luke/Roosevelt Hospital Center in New York, found that national fat-free brands were okay; but local products such as muffins, yogurt, and candy had fat counts eighty percent higher than advertised. During my ultra-distance cycling races, my sponsors supplied me with high dollar, high sugar, two hundred and twenty- five calorie bars which were a lot more convenient but a lot less nutritious, than a spaghetti dinner.

Staples In Your Cross–Training Eating Plan

Protein	Complex Carbohydrates	Vegetables
Egg whites	Potatoes	Asparagus
Chicken	Lima beans	Bamboo shoots
Ground Turkey	Black–eyed peas	Green beans
Turkey	Corn	Broccoli
Lean beef	Lentils	Brussels sprouts
Tuna	Oatmeal	Cabbage
Salmon	Peas	Carrots
Scallops	Popcorn	Cauliflower
Shrimp	Brown rice	Cucumbers
Halibut	Acorn squash	Eggplant
Other Fish	Sweet potato	Lettuce
Yogurt	Tomato	Red peppers
Skim milk	Shredded wheat	Green peppers
Cottage cheese	Yams	Spinach
Venison	White rice	Summer squash
Buffalo	Black beans	Zucchini squash
Pork loin	Kidney beans	Onions
Canadian bacon	Pinto beans	
Rabbit	Garbanzo beans	
	Split peas	
	Fruits	
	Cereals	
	Grains	
	Bagels	
	Breads	
	Crackers	
	Pasta	

Sweet Tooth

Be careful that your snack does not trigger a binge. I'm probably not the only one who has eaten a whole box of fat–free cookies in one sitting. An Oreo has two and three–tenths grams of fat per cookie while Snackwell's Devil's Food Cookie Cake is fat–free. Eating fat–free cookies left me feeling less guilty than gorging on a box of fat–laden ones, but that's a lot of calories. The following snacks may satisfy your sweet tooth or salt craving:

15 Satisfiers

1. Sugar–free gelatin
2. Sugar–free, fat–free pudding
3. Non–fat potato chips
4. Spicy flavored rice cakes
5. Non–fat tortilla chips dipped in salsa
6. Air–popped popcorn
7. Pretzels
8. Non–fat cookies
9. Sorbet
10. Sherbet
11. Non–fat frozen yogurt
12. Graham crackers
13. Vanilla wafers
14. Fig bars
15. Sugar–free popsicles

Low-Fat Snacks

1. 24 tortilla chips = 110 calories
2. 15 pretzel chips = 120 calories
3. 1 fat–free caramel corn cake = 50 calories
4. 13 reduced–fat mini chocolate chip cookies = 130 calories
5. 2 fat–free fig bars = 100 calories
6. 40 reduced–fat mini cheese crackers = 130 calories
7. 1 fat–free oatmeal raisin cookie = 100 calories
8. 2 honey graham crackers = 120 calories
9. 1 molasses cookie = 120 calories
10. 24 Teddy Grahams = 140 calories
11. 5 gingersnaps = 130 calories
12. 8 vanilla wafers = 140 calories

Cereals

Cereals are quick, convenient, nutritious, and delicious. Most cereals are a good source of carbohydrates. Many fortified cereals are high in fiber and vitamins. There are few high–fat cereals. Some add nuts and oils to their product to make each serving equal to the amount of fat contained in a pat of butter. But the culprit is sugar. Sugar Smacks, Cap'n Crunch, and Frosted Flakes contain between thirteen and fifteen grams of sugar per serving while Shredded Wheat contains zero grams. A bowl of puffed cereal floating in non–fat milk may only contain fifty calories per cup while a bowl of boulder–like cereal that sinks to the bottom may contain more than two hundred calories.

Meats

A study reported in the Archives of Internal Medicine demonstrated that lean beef may be as healthy as fish and chicken. Two groups were required to restrict their daily intake of saturated fats to ten percent. At the end of five weeks the beef group's cholesterol dropped eight percent and the chicken group's dropped ten percent. The leanest cuts of beef are sirloin tip, eye of round, and round steak. Pork center tenderloin and Canadian bacon are the leanest pork cuts. Small chickens are leaner than larger ones, and turkey breast is leaner than chicken. The least fatty fish are cod, flounder, haddock, scrod, halibut, shrimp, mussels, and lobster.

Cheese, Nuts and Seeds

The lowest fat cheeses are feta, farmers cheese, low-fat cottage cheese, and cream cheese made with low-fat yogurt. Cream cheese is eighty-five percent fat while low-fat cottage cheese is only twelve percent. Nuts, seeds, and peanut butter are eighty-five percent fat. Chestnuts are the least fat.

Suggested Herb Mixtures

Egg White Omelets, Salads, Vegetables, Fish, and **Meat**: 1/2 tsp. cayenne, 1 tbsp. garlic powder, 1 tsp. each ground thyme, basil, parsley, sage, savory, mace, onion powder, black pepper.

Vegetables and **Meat**: 1 tsp. thyme, marjoram, rosemary, and sage.

Fish: 3/4 tbsp. parsley, 1/2 tsp. onion powder and sage, 1/4 tsp. marjoram and paprika.

Meat, Vegetables and **Poultry**: 3/4 tsp. marjoram, 1/2 tsp. thyme, oregano, sage, and rosemary.

Meat, Potatoes, Vegetables: 1 tsp. dry mustard, 1/2 tsp. sage and thyme, and 1/4 tsp. marjoram.

Fish in tomato juice, dill, fennel, or thyme and chervil.

Beef in any of the following herbs: caraway, pickling spices, tarragon, marjoram, bay leaf (remove before serving), or chili powder.

Meat Loaf: add oregano, basil, garlic, or chili powder.

Chicken: add oregano, basil, garlic, chili powder, dry mustard, clove, or all-spice in different combinations to suit your taste.

Rice: try thyme, onion, paprika, or rosemary.

Cabbage is great with minced onion and nutmeg, caraway, vinegar, all-spice, or cloves.

Green Beans are good with dill, savory, onion, or tarragon.

Potatoes: for a new twist add caraway, onion, thyme, and parsley.

Zucchini: tarragon, basil, dill, oregano, or garlic.

Carrots: dill or Italian dressing.

As you experiment, you will find many other combinations.
Non–fat yogurt with horseradish, onion, chives, or dill, makes a great dip for raw vegetables.

Cabbage takes on a new taste if you shred and drop in boiling water for 2 – 3 minutes. Drain, add salt substitute, pepper, and a little powdered butter.

Fatty Foods To Avoid

1. **American cheese:** 75% calories from fat.

2. **Cream cheese:** 90% calories from fat.

3. **Pepperoni stick:** 80% calories from fat.

4. **Pork sausage:** 74% calories from fat.

5. **Spareribs:** 69% percent calories from fat.

Liquids

Approximately seventy percent of your body is water. Water is needed to digest and absorb food, transport nutrients, build and rebuild cells, remove waste products, and enhance circulation. Even without cross–training, your body loses a quart of fluid through the urine and two pints through the skin and lungs. Eight glasses of water are enough for a sedentary couch potato but not for a cross–trainer. Many cross–trainers are chronically dehydrated. Cross–trainers need about one milliliter of water per calorie expended. That means if you cross–train two–thousand calories, you need an additional two liters (two quarts or eight cups). Drink throughout the day. Try to drink eight ounces every hour. One study found that during a marathon, subjects drank only half the fluids they lost due to sweat. A one–percent drop in body weight can decrease blood volume by a quart, increasing heart rate and forcing the heart to work harder. For cross-trainers that can mean decreased performance. You can discover if you are dehydrated by monitoring the color of your urine. Light urine reflects adequate fluids. Darker urine reveals you need more fluids. If you drink enough water to support your cross–training, blood–sludgy effects of dehydration will be transformed into super–hydrated peak performance.

Carbohydrate Drinks

If you are cross–training in excess of two hours, research has demonstrated that carbohydrate sports drinks and juices can enhance your performance. A variety of sports drinks are on the market. Sometimes these drinks are too sugary so I dilute them with water. Look for a sports drink with between ten and twenty grams of carbohydrates per eight ounce serving (more carbohydrates than that decreases fluid absorption into the intestines). Make sure your drink has equal amounts of potassium and sodium (about fifty milligrams in an eight ounce serving). And enjoy the taste (you will drink it if you like it).

Non–Carbohydrate Drinks

Non–carbohydrate drinks that fit into your cross–training may include water, skim milk (whole milk is fifty percent fat, two percent milk gets thirty six percent of its calories from fat), and limited amounts of diet soda, coffee, and tea.

Prime the Pump

Your thirst mechanism may malfunction during cross–training. Body weight may drop a few pounds before you feel thirsty. I prime the pump by forcing myself to sip fluids while cycling. Contrary to the opinions of some health fanatics, it is not mandatory to drink pure water all of the time. Juices are ninety–five percent water, and oranges ninety percent. Also soups, grapes, and yogurt are mostly water. Coffee and tea are ninety–nine percent water, but the caffeine produces a moderate diuretic effect. Cross–train carrying a bottle filled with "the fluid of your choice" says Nancy Clark, MS., R.D., nutritionist at Sports Medicine, Brookline.

Alcohol

Alcohol has no fat, but it interferes with your fat burning metabolism. Your body will choose to oxidize alcohol instead of fat. Alcohol spares fat according to *Swiss Calorimetry Chamber Studies*. Ingesting alcohol is similar to consuming quantities of dietary fat. Cheryl Hartsough, R.D., says that if you are going to drink alcohol, drink a beer. And if you are going to drink a beer, drink a light beer with only one hundred calories.

Vitamins and Minerals

Some people believe they get all the vitamins and minerals they need in the foods they eat. I don't. In 1992 a University of California at Berkeley study showed that seventy–eight percent of people surveyed nationwide failed to consume two–thirds of the Recommended Dietary Allowance (RDA) of vitamins and minerals.

Free Radicals

CALL NOW !!!
1-800-US-UCKER

Cross–trainers probably don't get enough vitamins from food according to Beth Carlton, R.D. Exercise improves fitness but increases the number of free radicals in the body. Cross–trainers breathe a lot more air than non–exercisers, generating more free radicals. Free radicals are loose electrons in search of electron balance. Free electrons create more free radicals, damaging healthy tissue. Research demonstrated that animals exercised to exhaustion had three times the free radical concentration than normal.

Antioxidants

Vitamins C, E, and beta–carotene are vaporized by loose free radical electrons, sacrificing themselves for the benefit of organs and healthy tissue. I eat my share of vitamin C from foods which include: kale, watermelon, cauliflower, potatoes, broccoli, tomatoes, brussels sprouts, cabbage, red pepper, strawberry, cantaloupe, juice, and citrus fruit. But I rarely consume vitamin E rich asparagus, leafy greens, olives, seeds, margarine, wheat germ, nuts, or vegetable oil. Fortunately Beta–carotene filled foods are some of my favorites such as carrots, cantaloupe, pumpkin, red pepper, peaches, nectarines, papaya, mangos, apricots, spinach, sweet potatoes, and yellow squash.

Antioxidants and Other Vitamins

Antioxidant vitamin supplements have been shown to neutralize free radicals. I take anti–oxidant supplements daily. With my first meal I take a multivitamin with beta–carotene, four hundred international units of vitamin E, and five hundred milligrams of vitamin C. I take another five hundred milligrams of vitamin C at dinner.

Key Vitamins

Niacin – Raises High Density Lipoprotein (good cholesterol).

Folic Acid – Lowers cancer risk.

Vitamin B6, B12 – Lowers heart disease risk.

Vitamin D – Aids calcium absorption.

Copper – Helps keep your heart healthy.

Magnesium – Helps to lower blood pressure.

Zinc – Aids in immune function and wound healing.

Chromium – Helps our cells absorb blood sugar for energy.

Selenium, Vitamin E, C, Betacarotene – Antioxidants to prevent cancer and heart disease.

Calcium – Prevents osteoporosis.

Fish oil – Prevents heart disease, stroke, and some cancers.

Psyllium – A laxative.

Source: November 1994 *Prevention Magazine*

The following is a listing of important eating rules to incorporate into your everyday plans.

Eating Rules and Regulations

1. Under–eating or under–sleeping can cause over cross–training.

2. Schedule meals in advance.

3. Become sensitive to cross–training energy needs.

4. Do not skip meals.

5. Eat two servings of carbohydrates and one serving of protein at each meal.

6. Remember cross–eating and cross–training fuels your muscle.

7. Consume most of your calories early in the day.

8. Eat the right kind of foods.

9. Treat yourself to a "forbidden food" once a week.

10. Eat your high calorie foods in the morning.

11. Eating speeds up your metabolism.

12. A good late night snack is a high–fiber cereal with skim milk.

13. Craving sugar may mean that you are not eating enough protein and carbohydrates throughout the day.

14. Take control of your cravings by fueling your body every few hours.

15. Special order low–fat at restaurants. Use tomato, broth, and wine–based sauces instead of high–fat gravy, cream, and cheese sauces.

16. Buy large quantities of brown rice, oatmeal, tuna, potatoes, and large bags of chicken breasts, vegetables, and cereal when they are on sale.

17. Make small changes: Skim milk instead of regular, jelly on toast instead of butter, mustard on sandwiches instead of mayonnaise, diet soda nstead of regular, non–fat frozen desserts instead of high–fat frozen yogurt, use non–fat salad dressing, and eat your chicken without the skin.

18. Diet sodas don't satisfy a craving. Choose a non–fat snack instead.

19. If you miss the potato chip crunch, choose crackers, cauliflower, broccoli, peppers, carrots, celery, baked tortilla chips, saltines, matzos, or non–fat crackers.

20. Beware of chef salads and Caesar salad.

21. If you are hungry, start your meal with a non–fat soup.

22. Schedule a reasonable after dinner mini–meal instead of succumbing to an uncontrolled binge.

23. Don't eat fewer than one thousand calories each day.

(To lose body–fat see Nutrition Chart B on page 27.)

Chart **B**

NUTRITION

Food	Date	Time Eaten	Calories	Fat Grams	Feelings

CROSS-TRAINING

3

STRENGTH

Stronger is Better

More muscle means a faster metabolism which requires more food for energy. A high metabolism is a blessing in our over–fed, under–exercised lifestyle. Centuries ago slabs of muscle combined with low body fat would have been anathema. Our hunter–gatherer ancestors survived long periods without food. Today with our over–abundance, low body fat and rock–hard muscle signify health and vitality. Muscle is not just cosmetic. Muscles help us walk, keep our balance, catch ourselves if we fall, and then pick ourselves up. In the revised guidelines the American College of Sports Medicine (ACSM) recommends that strength training be an integral part of an adult fitness program. Weight–trained men and women generally have better reaction times, increased flexibility, endurance, and leaner body mass than non–lifters. Circuit weight training lowers blood pressure and increases food transit time through the colon to combat some types of cancer.

Specificity of Training

Some people need muscles that are good for carrying bricks up and down ladders. Others prefer hoisting seventy pound bales of hay. To improve your brick–carrying muscles, move briskly through a variety of exercises on a training circuit. To launch a bale of hay, rest two minutes between each heavy power set. Resistance training will enhance raking, housework, mowing the lawn, and house–painting while protecting your joints and spine.

Calisthenics

You can push and pull your own body weight using calisthenics. Push-ups, pull-ups, squat-thrusts, crunches, and leg lifts are but a few of the many exercises you can perform. No equipment is necessary and the exercises are easy to do.

Free Weights

Power lifters and bodybuilders use free weights primarily because they require the use of stabilizer muscles. Stabilizer muscles help to balance the weights through the full range of motion. Free weights are relatively inexpensive and are found in many home gyms.

Machine Weights

Machine weights are safer than free weights because you do not have to balance them. To change the weight you simply use a selector pin. Disadvantages include cost, size, and a restricted range of motion.

Resistance Tubing

If you do not have access to free weights or machine weights, tubing is okay. Tubing is inexpensive and portable, but it is difficult to measure progress.

Starting a Program

A stronger athlete is a better athlete. Resistance training can increase your strength, muscular endurance, and metabolism. The key to improving your strength and muscular endurance is training smart.

Tips for Smart Training

1. Train with resistance equipment for an hour two to four times a week

2. Train each muscle group a maximum of twice a week.

3. Ease into your workout. Choose a weight that you can comfortably control.

4. Start with some easy repetitions, then gradually increase the intensity.

5. Perform one exercise per body part.

6. Work the large muscle groups of the legs, back, and chest first.

7. Stretch each muscle group following each set.

8. Breathe normally during an exercise. If you are exerting, however, exhale during the contraction. Inhale on your short rests between each contraction.

9. Maintain good posture: keep your stomach in, relax your neck, keep your back flat (don't arch).

10. Focus your concentration on a specific muscle group. Feel the weight in every repetition.

11. The amount of weight you lift should never compromise your form. For example, to train your chest and triceps, focus on the pectoral muscles in your chest. Concentrate on pushing with the triceps muscles in the back of your arm.

12. Explode into your movement with a controlled, one hundred percent energized effort.

13. Move the weight through a full range of motion.

14. Imagine a surge of power as the blood enters the working muscle.

15. Relax your entire body except for the muscle groups you are working. If you are working your triceps, attempt to keep your facial muscles relaxed.

16. If your muscles are growing larger, stronger, and more flexible and you are not gaining additional body fat, you are doing everything right.

Muscular Endurance

If your goal is to improve muscular endurance, work your large muscle groups in rapid succession. You will see improvement after approximately five weeks. Keep charts to record your progress. If you are a thin person (ectomorph), you need less recovery time than a muscular individual (mesomorph) or a person who carries more body fat (endomorph).

Strength Training

Your muscles will adapt to heavier weight over time. Increase the amount of weight you are lifting gradually. Be patient. Do not work a muscle if it is sore from a previous workout. As you increase the weight, you will increase size and strength. For maximum strength gain, do six repetitions. Each repetition will be so intense you should reach exhaustion by the sixth.

High Intensity

To continue to stimulate muscle growth, you must add intensity to your workout. Resistance training must be done high intensity to do any good, says William Evans, Ph.D. Do both high repetition–light weight and low repetition–heavy weight to stimulate slow–twitch and fast–twitch muscle fibers. We all have both slow and fast–twitch fibers in different combinations throughout our bodies. To increase intensity you can choose to increase the number of sets, repetitions, or the amount of weight you are lifting. Or you may decrease your rest–time between sets.

Principles to Increase Intensity

In the November 1994 issue of *Muscle & Fitness*, Joe Weider makes the following suggestions:

1. **Progressive Overload:** Gradually increase the amount of weight you lift on a weekly basis.

2. **Isolation:** Isolate a specific muscle rather than allowing auxiliary muscles to take part in the movement.

3. **Muscle Confusion:** Vary your exercises, sets, and repetitions so your muscles never completely adjust to the stress.

4. **Priority:** Train your weakest body part first.

5. **Pyramid:** Add weight and decrease repetitions between sets until you make your maximum lift.

6. **Split system:** Split your body parts into different workouts so you can train each muscle group twice a week.

7. **Flushing:** Pumping blood to a specific body part and keep the blood there by doing several different exercises to target that area.

8. **Supersets:** Work antagonistic muscles consecutively such as biceps and triceps or quadriceps and hamstring.

9. **Compound sets:** Do two sets of exercises back to back, working the same muscle group.

10. **Holistic training:** Do a variety of repetitions from low to high.

11. **Cycle training:** During different parts of the year, focus on different parts of your body with different levels of intensity to add variety and prevent injury.

12. **Isotension training:** Consciously flex your muscle throughout the repetition.

13. **Cheating:** Let your free hand help your working arm lift the weight so you can muscle it down slow and with control.

14. **Tri-sets:** Do three exercises for the same muscle group in rapid succession.

15. **Giant sets:** Do a series of four to six exercises for one muscle group.

16. **Pre-exhaustion:** Work a muscle in its primary motion to a point of fatigue, then do a different exercise to fatigue the muscle.

17. **Rest-pause:** Take between thirty and ninety seconds to rest between repetitions in order to handle a heavy weight.

18. **Continuous tension:** Train slow and deliberately, maintaining constant tension on your muscles throughout the entire range of motion.

19. **Negative-training:** Have your training partner lift the weight to you. Then you resist it on the way down.

20. **Forced repetitions:** At the end of your set, when you are unable to continue, have your partner ease you through your sticking point to get a few extra repetitions.

21. **Double split:** Work one body part in the morning and another in the evening.

22. **Triple split:** Work one body part in the morning, another in the afternoon, and a third in the evening.

23. **Burns:** Do three to six partial movements at the end of your regular set, bringing extra blood and lactic acid into the working muscle.

24. **Bombing and blitzing:** Combine any of the above principles used in succession until you reach muscular failure.

25. **Speed:** Explode into your repetitions on your heavy sets, developing speed and power by stimulating white, fast twitch muscle fibers.

26. **Quality training:** Reduce the time you take for rest between sets.

27. **Instinctive:** Discover which priciples work best for you, then do them.

Age is Not a Factor

It's a myth that your body doesn't respond to exercise as you grow older. Muscle loss is not an inevitable part of growing old, says William Evans, Ph.D. His research demonstrated that muscles get stronger in response to weight training at any age.

Listen to Your Body

Individualize your strength program to meet your changing needs and goals. Plan the order of your exercises and the intensity of your training system. Train yourself to "feel" your workouts. Some days train until you cannot do another repetition while other days concentrate on perfect form. Too many hard training days can increase cortisol which is catabolic (destructive) to your muscles and detrimental to your immune system. Straddle the fine line between a great workout and overtraining.

Lifting to Lose

Lift weights to lose body fat. Lifting weights increases your lean muscle mass. The more lean muscle on your body, the more calories you burn. One pound of muscle burns about seventy–five extra calories a day according to D. Maxwell, president of Maxercise Sports Fitness Center. If you gain three pounds of muscle, you can eat an extra one hundred thirty–five calories daily.

Muscle Increases Metabolism

There's only so much fat you can take off by dieting and doing cardiovascular exercises, says Wayne Wescott, Ph.D., fitness director. Strength training adds lean muscle, increasing your metabolism. Tufts University researcher Wayne Campbell put twenty–four senior citizens on a weight–lifting program for twelve weeks. Their food was monitored; and, in order to stabilize their weight, all lifters were required to consume three hundred extra calories each day. According to Campbell, without the additional food, his subjects would have lost an average of ten pounds because their metabolic rates increased by about seven percent.

Metabolism Booster

After the age of thirty, metabolic rate decreases five–tenths of a percent per year in response to diminishing muscle mass. Rosenberg and Evans coined the term "sarcopenia" for losing muscle due to inactivity as we age. Wescott said that unexercised muscle is lost at a rate of about one–half pound per year in adults. This loss decreases resting metabolism, possibly resulting in gaining fat. If you lose muscle and continue to eat the same foods, the calories that supported your muscle will be stored as fat. The average American adds about a pound of body fat each year. Maintain your muscle and you won't have to cut calories in mid–life.

Endocrinologist, Jorge Calles says that a cross–trainer can over–eat occasionally and not gain body fat because his metabolism naturally adjusts. However a non–exerciser's metabolism slows down in response to a binge.

Quicker Response

Roberta Rikli, Ph.D., professor of kinesiology, reported in the March 1994 issue of Research Quarterly that strong muscles reacted quicker than flabby ones. Forty–four women hit a foot pad when a signal was given. Those with the strongest leg muscles reacted the fastest. Toned muscles have more nerve fibers and blood vessels to help the impulse get from thought to action.

Body–Fat Analysis

Measure your muscle to body fat ratio by underwater weighing, skinfold calipers, bioelectrical impedance, or ultra–sound. A recent study by R. Stout in *Medicine In Science In Sports and Exercise* concluded that underwater weighing was the most valid and reliable measure-ment device. The next best was skinfold calipers. Bioelectrical impedance and ultra–sound tended to overestimate fat in lean individuals and underestimate fat in the obese. In any of these measures the key to a successful reading is the ability of the technician. Be sure to use the same technician under the same testing conditions each time you test. Minimum body fat for a male is three percent and twelve percent for a female.

Waist–to–Hip

Another popular way to measure body fat stores is to measure waist–to–hip ratios. The waist measurement is taken at the point of smallest circumference while the hip measurement is taken at the point of greatest circumference. Most men are shaped like apples, with their body fat stored in the waist, while women resemble pears, having a higher percentage of fat stored in the thighs. "Apples", or central obesity, is strongly correlated with fat that is packed around our internal organs and is the most lethal, creating a higher risk for heart disease. If men have a waist–to–hip ratio of one or higher, they should attempt to lose body fat. Women need to lose fat if their ratio is eighty percent or more.

Air Displacement

Body fat may be measured by sitting in an air displacement chamber. Simply sit in the air displacement chamber for twenty seconds. It uses air displacement to determine metabolic rate, percent lean weight, and body fat. The chamber costs twenty thousand dollars.

Let's Do It

If you decide to lift weights at home, you need a bench (a picnic bench will be okay), and several sets of dumbells. A mirror can help keep your form, and music may improve motivation. Do three sets of ten repetitions of each of the following exercises. Take two seconds to raise the weight and three seconds to lower it. If you are time limited, do one set of each exercise consecutively in a circuit training approach, starting from a standing position, then seated, and finishing on your back. If you have thirty minutes, you can perform three sets of the following Compound–Consecutive–Circuit program. Change the intensity of your exercises every six months. When using the following program, refer to the drawing below detailing the major muscles of the body.

Major Muscles of the Body

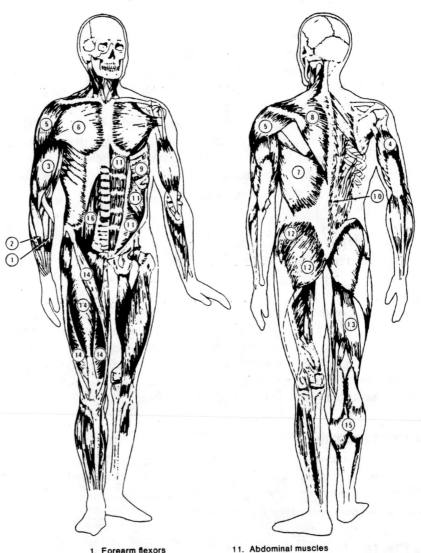

1. Forearm flexors
2. Brachioradialis
3. Biceps
4. Triceps
5. Deltoid
6. Pectoral muscles
7. Latissimus dorsi
8. Trapezius
9. Serratus anterior
10. Erector spinae
    (spinal extensors)
11. Abdominal muscles
    a. Internal and exter-
       nal obliques
    b. Rectus abdominis
    c. Transversalis
12. Gluteal muscles
13. Hamstrings
14. Quadriceps muscles
15. Gastrocnemius, soleus
    muscles
16. Iliopsoas (under ab-
    dominal muscles)

Compound–Consecutive Circuit

A) Standing "7" (page 37)
B) Seated "6" (page 44)
C) Lying "5" (page 50)

A) Standing "7"

1. **Bent Over Row** (lat. work latissimus dorsi; back): While bending from the waist, keep your head up and bend your knees and grasp the dumbells in an overhand grip with your hands a little more than shoulder width apart. Keep your torso parallel to the floor and pull the dumbells up toward your chest, keeping your elbows close against your body. Maintain a flat back, and lower the dumbells in a straight line back towards the floor.

---

2. **<u>Reverse Curl</u>** (forearms; biceps): Grip the dumbells at thigh level with an overhand grip, hands a little less than shoulder width apart. Bring the arms up from the waist to shoulder level until your biceps touch your forearms. Lower the weights back down to your thighs using your elbows as the fulcrum.

3. **Arm Curl** (biceps): Grasp the dumbells in an underhand grip, palms up, arms close to your sides. Allow the dumbells to rest against your thighs. Pull the dumbells toward your chin in a semicircle until your forearms touch your biceps. Keep your wrist locked. Lower the dumbells on the same path you lifted them. Move the weights up and down slowly through the full range of motion.

4. **<u>Frontal Deltoid</u>** (shoulder): Grab the dumbells with your hands about shoulder width apart and your palms facing downward in front of your thighs. Keep your knees and elbows slightly bent, and slowly raise the dumbells toward your head. Pause when your arms are parallel to the floor, and slowly lower them back towards your thighs.

5. **Trapezius Training** (upper shoulder): Grab the dumbells with your palms facing downward, your hands together, and your arms extended so that the dumbells rest against your thighs. Bring the dumbells up toward your chin while leading with the elbows so that they flare out to the sides up to your ears. Keep constant tension throughout the full range of motion as the dumbells remain close to your body. At the top of the movement pause and flex your trapezius muscles.

6. **More Traps** (shoulder shrugs): Grasp the dumbells with an overhand grip, your hands shoulder width apart, and your arms down to your sides. Keep your elbows straight as you droop your shoulders down as far as you can and then raise them as high as you can up to your ears with the weight providing resistance in both directions.

CROSS-TRAINING

7. **Half–Squats** (quadriceps): Stand with a dumbell in each hand, arms extended down to your side. With your feet shoulder width apart slowly bend your knees until your upper thighs reach a forty–five degree angle. Pause and straighten up again. Keep your head up and your back straight.

B) Seated "6"

1. <u>**Triceps Kickbacks**</u> (triceps): While on your hands and knees grasp a dumbell with one hand with your elbow at a ninety degree angle. Extend your arm straight back until your elbow is locked. Hold for one second then return to the ninety degree angle. Repeat with your other arm.

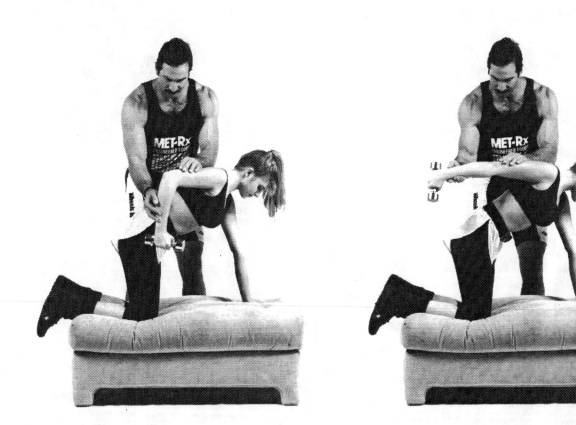

2. **Single–Handed Lat. Work** (latissimus dorsi): Grab the dumbell with one hand while the same knee is braced on a bench. Extend the arm as far down as you can toward your side and feel a pulling sensation in your lats. Then lift the dumbell to your hip as the resistance presses down. Reverse hands and make sure to move through a full range of motion.

3. **Shoulder Press** (deltoid; triceps): Sit on a bench with good posture, holding the dumbells on the back of your shoulders. With the dumbells in an overhand grip, press them toward the ceiling as the resistance presses down. Keep your torso and head in a straight line with your chest out. Push with equal pressure from each arm upward to full extension. As you lower the dumbells toward your shoulders, keep constant tension.

4. **One–Armed Curls** (biceps): Grip the dumbell with your right hand as the left hand supports the right arm to isolate the tension in the biceps. Lift and lower the bar through the full range of motion while moving the bar at a semi–circular angle with the elbow joint as the fulcrum.

5. **More Triceps Work** (triceps): Sit on the bench holding one dumbell behind your neck. Extend the bar upward as the resistance presses downward until your arm is straight. Feel the tension in the back of the arm. Let the resistance provide pressure in both directions. Switch hands and repeat.

6. **Shoulder Flies** (deltoids): Sit with a dumbell in each hand. Lead with your elbows as you lift them parallel to the floor, working the lateral aspect of your shoulders. Slowly raise your arms upward. The weight should provide tension in both directions.

C) Lying "5"

1. **Bench Flies** (pectoral; triceps): Lie on your back on a bench, grasp the dumbells in an overhand grip, and extend your arms from your chest level upwards. Have enough weight to provide tension so you can keep the dumbells moving smoothly and evenly. Keep your elbows slightly bent through the full range of motion. Feel your chest and triceps working. Keep the back of your head, buttocks, and lower back in contact with the bench. Arching your back takes the pressure off the chest and triceps.

2. **Pullovers** (latissimus dorsi; chest): Lie on your back and grip the dumbell with both hands. Extend the dumbell back over your head as the bar dumbell provides resistance. Then flex it back in the opposite direction. Feel a stretch in your upper back and chest.

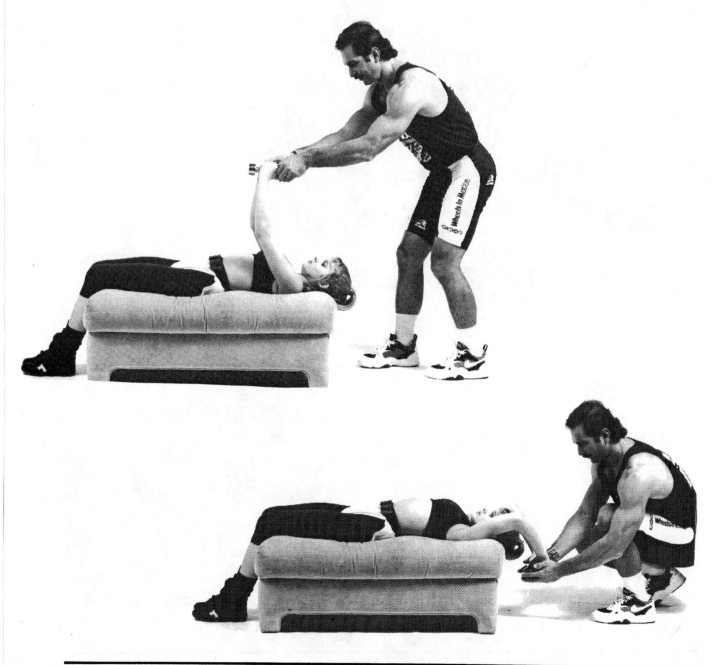

3. **Posterior Raises** (rear deltoids): Lie on your stomach and grip one dumbell in each hand. Raise the dumbells from the floor until they are a few inches above parallel. Then slowly lower them back towards the floor. Keep your elbows bent for the duration of the exercise.

4. **Lateral Raises** (lateral deltoids): Lie on your side holding one dumbell with your top hand. Raise the dumbell from the floor up to a vertical position and then slowly lower it back towards the floor. Repeat with your other arm.

5. **<u>Triceps Extensions</u>** (triceps): Lie on your back holding one dumbell in your right hand. Extend the dumbell into a vertical position and then slowly lower it back towards your left shoulder. Repeat with your left hand.

(To chart your weight training performance see Strength Chart C on page 55.)

Chart

STRENGTH

Dumbell Compound–Consecutive–Circuit

	Day	Time	Reps.	Intensity	Weight
Bent Over Row					
Bench press					
Arm curl					
Shoulder press					
Reverse curl					
One–armed curls					
One–armed lat.					
Pullovers					
Triceps extensions					
Close grip bench					
Frontal deltoid					
Upright rows					
Shoulder shrugs					
Shoulder flies					
Bench flies					
Squats					
Deadlifts					
Lunges					
Posterior raises					
Lateral raises					
Triceps extensions					

4

POWER

In the Zone

Variety

Heading to the gym on leg day can be depressing. Squats, lunges, deadlifts, hack squats, leg extensions, leg curls, and calf raises aren't fun. Recently I strained a muscle in my back doing deadlifts. I was daydreaming instead of focusing on my hamstrings. As Arnold Schwartzenegger said, when you get bored with your workout or when your muscles stop growing, you "shock them". So once a week instead of going to the gym on leg day, I cross–train my lower body with power–plyometrics!

Acceleration

Olympic sprinters and triple–jumpers don't have scrawny legs. One reason is they do plyometrics. Plyometrics combines speed and strength to improve explosiveness. The object is to generate the greatest amount of force in the shortest amount of time. Power is a key component of football, basketball, karate, tennis, and most track events. These sports require both force and speed. When a karate practitioner breaks a board, it's not just how hard he hits it but how fast. Training for power combines strength training and plyometrics. Plyometrics consists of a variety of drills that increase your strength, size, and power. The bounding action attempts to take advantage of the stretch–recoil and stretch–reflex properties of muscles. The quick stretch applied to the muscle during push–off is thought to increase muscle contraction, thereby enhancing explosiveness. These different exercises involve involuntary neuromuscular contractions controlled by the central nervous system. Unlike normal weight lifting plyometrics requires you to accelerate through a full range of motion and then relax into a full stretch. After a few months of lower body plyometrics your weight workouts will seem easier. Not only will you get stronger but your anaerobic threshold will increase so you can rest less between sets. You won't be huffing and puffing on supersets.

Plyometrics Builds Fast–Twitch Fibers

Speaking of huffing and puffing, remember the time you sprinted to catch that guy who stole your wallet? Or when you took your eye off the road to scarf down pizza and ran over an innocent bystander, forcing you to deadlift your three–thousand–pound car setting a new world record? Dream on! I'm not going to say cross–training with plyometrics will transform you into your favorite super–hero, but plyometrics will build your fast–twitch muscle fibers. Plyometrics pre-stretches your fast–twitch fibers followed by a full–range explosive muscular contraction. Researchers say fast–twitch (white, type II) fibers grow readily in response to high–intensity, short–duration, anaerobic movements such as heavy weight training or plyometrics.

Genetics

Let's find out whether you have more fast–twitch muscle fibers like Carl Lewis or more slow–twitch (red, type I) muscle fibers like me. First we gouge a thimble of muscle tissue from your thigh, leaving you screaming in a bloody heap. Then we'll examine this biopsy–plug under a microscope and start counting. An easier way for you to guesstimate your ratio of slow–twitch/fast–twitch fibers would be to decide whether you're more efficient at a one–repetition maximum squat or doing thirty repetitions at thirty percent of your maximum. And don't think because you finished a marathon that your arms are predominantly slow–twitch. Genetics may bless you with a mostly fast–twitch upper body and extra slow–twitch fibers below the waist. When I began cycling, I hoped I would be a fast–fiber sprinter so I could race short sprints and win lots of money. To my chagrin I own the legs of a slow–twitch turtle requiring me to race in ultra marathons that last days on end and offer little prize money.

Do It All

Regardless of your predominant fiber type, researchers are unsure if muscle fibers grow in size (hypertrophy) or if muscle cells proliferate (hyperplasia) in response to resistance training and plyometrics. Until we know for sure I'm going to play it safe and do both heavy weight and high–repetition training one day a week and cross–train with plyometrics on my other leg day. There is no sweeter residual soreness than exploding through ten sets of plyometrics.

No Pain

I have modified my plyometric program so you do not need any special equipment. The only requirements are a cushioned floor or a nice soft back yard and a good pair of shoes. Don't wear those ratty old tennis shoes you use to mow the lawn. If you attempt plyometrics on a cement floor, don't sue me when you injure your knees and shins. Your ankles, knees, and lower back must be in perfect condition. No joint pain is gain.

Start Easy

When you begin plyometric training, jump no more than two inches high. Do plyometrics in secret. If anyone sees you, they may suspect an overdose of caffeine. It's a sure bet you'll be wheezing like a ninety year old upon the completion of each set. If so, take at least a minute between plyometric sets to let your heart rate settle down. You will be happier the next morning if you perform just one set of each exercise. If you think you're in great shape, repeat the circuit; but don't blame me. I told you one set was enough. If you feel wasted, you are normal. Be thankful you can walk. After a month of training, you may do plyometrics in public and increase the height of your jumps by one inch a month. You can gradually increase to three sets of twenty reps. Because of joint stress, perform plyometrics a maximum of once a week.

Jump Rope

Warm up thoroughly before you start plyometrics. Jump rope; then stretch. Never jump on concrete. Look for wood floors, rubber floors, or rubber tiles. Jump lightly on the balls of your feet with your knees bent to make your calves work and take the pressure off your shins and knees. Use your wrists to turn the rope. Hold your hands at your waist about two inches from your body. Jump low.

Psycho–Plyometrics

As soon as I throw my rope down (like Stallone in Rocky), I do some light stretching while I mentally prepare for some plyometric power training. Perform plyometrics in the theater of your mind. Close your eyes prior to each set. Take thirty seconds to see, feel, and experience each jump. Do not permit negative thoughts. If you are in the middle of an exercise and you think, "I'm tired. Not one more jump.", immediately think, "I was tired, but my legs are springs bounding higher and higher and higher."

Set 1

Ten Consecutive Jumps: Jump ten times without stopping. Land on the balls of your feet and bend your knees to 90 degrees and roll to your heels. Then roll to the balls of your feet and then do it again.

Set 2

Lunge Jumps: Begin in a forward lunge position. Jump up and switch stances in the air so each foot replaces the other. Take no rest between jumps.

Set 3

Jump, Alternate Knee: Raise your right knee forcefully, coming off the floor. Let your left leg follow your right leg as you are airborne (kind of like a karate jump front kick). Fall softly to the floor, rolling from the balls of your feet to your heels. Repeat, beginning with your left leg. Perform ten consecutive jumps, alternating knees each jump.

Set 4

Superman Jump: Take a three–step running start and bound off both feet, throwing your arms in the air (like Superman jumping out a window). After landing, take three steps back and continue for ten repetitions.

Set 5

Jump, Clap Your Feet: Begin with your feet a little less than shoulder width apart. Jump up and touch your feet together (penguin style), then land solidly in your original position. Do ten repetitions.

Set 6

Hands to Knees: Jump up, bringing your knees up to your hands. Try to keep your knees together. Do ten repetitions.

Set 7

    Heels to Hips: Jump and bring your heels toward your hips. Be careful of your knees. Do ten repetitions.

Set 8

    Fingers Touch: Touch your fingers to the floor and bound up as high as you can. Do ten repetitions.

Set 9

Breakfall: Roll onto your back and slap the floor with the palms of your hands. Rise to a standing position as quickly as you can without using your arms. Be careful of your knees. Do ten repetitions.

Set 10

Squat Thrusts: Bend your knees and waist so that your hands touch the floor. Throw your feet straight back so that you are now in a push-up position. Immediately drive your feet back toward your hands to your original squat position. Stand up as quickly as you can. Repeat ten times.

Cool Down

After you're done, stretch thoroughly and then cool down with some light jump rope. Be prepared for some soreness for the next couple of days. Do plyometrics outdoors for a change of pace. Feel the breeze and the sun. If you are a morning person, cross–train before work. If you enjoy evening training, fly high after dinner. Any time is a good time. If you lose your motivation for plyometrics, re-evaluate your goals, increase your intensity, upgrade your diet, sleep more, or decrease your frequency. Your recovery time and your nutrition are as important as your plyometric cross–training.

(To chart your plyometric performance see Chart D on page 67.)

PLYOMETRICS

	Time	Date	Reps	Feelings
Set 1 Ten consecutive jumps				
Set 2 Lunge jumps				
Set 3 Jump, alternate knee				
Set 4 Superman jump				
Set 5 Jump, clap your feet				
Set 6 Hands to knees				
Set 7 Heels to hips				
Set 8 Fingers touch				
Set 9 Breakfall				
Set 10 Squat thrusts				

5

FOCUS

Body/Mind

Did you catch the mini–series, The Heart Of Healing, with Jane Seymour? After falling in love with Dr. Quinn, I recall her persuading us that our minds can heal our bodies using pac–man like macrophage visualizations to swallow up cancer cells. Deepak Chopra, M.D., shares in his seminars that every thought we hold affects every cell in our body and in turn our state of wellness. An anorexic looks into a mirror and sees a fat person. A bodybuilder focuses on his skinny calves.

Gaining control over the thoughts and images we hold in our minds can make the difference between success and failure, life and death. The mind will be integrally involved with the body in the future of medicine according to Larry Dossey, M.D., chairman of the National Institute of Health's Alternative Medicine Division. One of his patients was diagnosed with countless tumors in his chest with little hope for recovery. A year later his X–rays were clear. The only intervention was round–the–clock prayer.

Prayer

We've heard of faith healing, but Dr. Dossey took the power of prayer into the realm of science. An experimenter prayed over a petri dish filled with bacteria. The bacteria grew bigger and stronger than bacteria in a forlorn control dish! Candace Pert, Ph.D., said that chemical processes mediate emotion within our brains and on the surfaces of every cell in the body.

Everybody's Doing It

Whisper, "I pray cross–training makes me better." Arnold imagined oxygenated blood nourishing damaged fibers. Kwai Chang Kane meditated while doing dynamic tensionexercises. Sport psychologist Dr. Jim Loehr requires his

THE WISE MAN WALKS WITH HEAD BOWED.

players to act "as if" they are strong. Anthony Clark, reputedly the world's strongest man, believes his power comes directly from God. Frank Zane, champion bodybuilder, uses bizarre devices to synchronize his brain waves.

Belief

According to David Phillips, Ph.D., what you believe can have a tremendous effect on your health and performance. His studies demonstrate that seriously ill people can postpone dying for certain occasions or decisions. He suggests we should invent mental health clubs to exercise a better attitude. Friends, clubs, activities, and efforts can allow you to feel cheerful. Go out of your way to keep yourself in pleasant surroundings.

Relaxation

Anxiety

The opposite of being relaxed is feeling anxious. When anxiety becomes unbearable, our hormones respond to a perceived threat. This primitive device termed the fight or flight response, was originally useful for survival. Whenever we fear looking bad, not meeting expectations, or losing, we tighten up; and our cross–training efforts are sometimes negated. Symptoms manifest themselves in stomach butterflies, debilitating thought processes, shortness of breath, and confusion. Responses to these symptoms include trying too hard, rushing, and making mistakes. Performance anxiety applies to cross–training as well as speeches. Whether it's interviews or in–laws, stomachs tighten and palms sweat. You're not yourself. You say things you don't mean. You're stiff. You don't look comfortable. You try to smile, but it's an obvious charade.

Stress

When the body is under stress, hormones spew into the blood, increasing blood pressure, blood sugar, heart rate, and muscle tension. These conditions continue long after the psychological stress has abated. We become accustomed to stress but that does not change its impact on our system.

Cortisol

Car phones, computers, and fax machines keep us working all the time thereby increasing cortisol levels, decreasing our ability to relax and retain muscle. High cortisol levels exert a catabolic effect on muscles, bone, and connective tissue. Cortisol increases blood pressure and decreases rapid eye movement (REM) sleep. Marielle Rebuffe–Scrive, Yale psychologist, found that uncontrolled stress in rats increased their level of cortisol production.

Relaxation and Cortisol

Should you lock the door, unplug the phone, turn off the fax, and meditate to achieve peak cross–training performance? Relaxation strategies can decrease cortisol production. Cortisol inhibits muscle growth and can decrease your training effect. Herbert Benson, M.D., president of the Mind/Body Medical Institute, advises that all formal relaxation techniques dampen the stress–induced production of cortisol.

Priorities

Dr. Mihalyi Csikszentmihalyi suggests to reduce stress: note the things that are important, then watch the things you spend your time doing. Cut back on activities that don't fit your priorities. Try to make your routine more enjoyable. We choose to be frantic. We try to make lots of money, hang glide, write books, learn to play guitar, and be in great shape.

Relaxed Concentration

Another antidote to life–stress is a relaxed focus. Relaxation and proper concentration helps you feel in control. Replace apprehension with tenacity; view cross–training as a challenge. The following are a few methods to channel unwanted anxiety into a positive cross–training performance:

1. Ask yourself what could be so important to cause you to waste half your day fretting. If the cross–training event is truly anxiety provoking, go to step two.

2. Understand that every cross–trainer gets butterflies.

3. Take a deep breath from your diaphragm and relax cross–training muscles that feel tense.

4. Visualize yourself appearing comfortably focused and prepared for your impending cross–training performance.

5. When your imagined cross–training performance begins, "see" everything going as planned.

6. Imagine a glitch in your cross–training, but see yourself smiling, recovering fully and completely.

7. Be spontaneous. Your relaxation will allow you to be more flexible, providing for a better cross–training performance.

8. Don't focus so much on yourself. Other people don't care as much about you as you do.

9. Empathize with the anxiety of your cross–training comrades. Help relieve their burden by relaxing.

10. Take control of yourself; be brave.

Relaxation

Sit with your back straight and take a deep breath from your diaphragm, then exhale. Relax. Focus only on your breath. Let nothing else distract or disturb you, just breathe. When any distracting thoughts or sounds interfere, just let them go in one ear and out the other as you go deeper relaxed. Close this book, close your eyes, and continue your relaxation. After you feel five minutes has passed, glance at your watch and then slowly come out of your relaxed state. Or, close your eyes and continue your relaxation. Warning – do not lie down unless your goal is sleep.

Visualization

How many hours do you spend actively cross–training each week? Do you think the mental aspect of cross–training is important? How many hours do you spend mentally preparing for cross–training each week? Your mind can program your body for peak cross–training performance. Your body will respond quickly when your brain directs your training. Mind–body training is most effective when you are relaxed. To improve your cross–training, focus on your activity during twilight stages before sleep and as you awaken. If you are cross–training for tennis, imagine a cat–quick, killer volley. Own an awesome forehand. Plan strategy during idle moments. Focus on your serve while listening to a boring lecture or driving. Be careful not to career off the side of a mountain while mentally acing your opponent. Penn State researcher, Bruce Hale, Ph.D., discovered that his biceps exhibited significant electrical activity just by thinking about flexing them!

Virtual Realization

Virtual reality (VR) headsets simulate your movements on a computer. Pedal faster on your VR ergometer and enjoy a whoosh of air. Until you can afford a VR exercise machine, use a less expensive version I call virtual realization. Psychologist David Marks claims that mental practice must be a visual, auditory, olfactory, sensory, and emotional exercise to detail a complete experience.

Virtual Realization: Cross–Training with Weights

1. Soften your gaze. Imagine your cross–training workout isabout to begin.

2. Take a moment to see, feel, and experience each repetition.

3   Pick up the bar and begin.

4. It may be difficult to narrow your attention but "focus–in" during your lift.

5. Hear the clang of the weights.

6. Feel your Z–bands splitting and proliferating. Satellite cells are nourishing torn muscle fibers. Notice a surge of power as the blood enters your working muscle.

7. Explode into each movement with a controlled, one hundred percent effort as you squeeze out each repetition.

8. Send blood to the working body part to keep the pump.

Mind/Body Champion

Target shooters, basketball free throw shooters, tennis servers, track athletes, skiers, bodybuilders, power lifters, and other cross–trainers swear by the power of mental rehearsal. Virtual realization allows you to see, feel, and experience yourself as well as to direct your thoughts. Try virtual realization to improve your cross–training. Do it anytime, anywhere. Only you know what transpires between your ears. Whether you meditate, do biofeed-back, or pray, there is an undeniable link between your mind–set and your cross–training.

Do Something

Dr. Dossey, Far Eastern mystics, and positive thinkers teach that a few minutes of focused attention can have a tremendously beneficial effect on your cross–training lifestyle. George Solomon, M.D., professor of psychiatry at UCLA, claims that different behaviors give people a sense of control. Whether a person meditates or prays, taking active control is the opposite of helplessness.

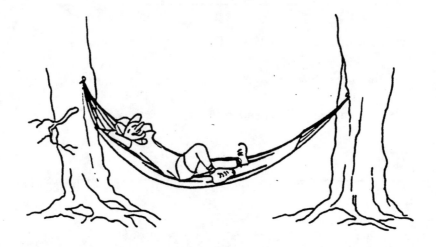

Spiritual Cross–Training

Most of us neglect our spiritual exercises. Sometimes we forget. Dr. Dossey says to pray for a positive outcome. The Bible says pray without ceasing, pray for God's will, and believe that God has already granted your prayer. An open–ended prayer combined with a focused, clear, and controlled image of God's will form a spiritual approach to achieving your cross–training dreams.

(To chart your focusing skills see Relaxation-Visualization-Prayer Chart E on page 75.)

RELAXATION-VISUALIZATION-PRAYER

Date	Time	Duration	Focus	Feelings

6

STRETCHING

The Key to Success

Everyone Can Stretch

Bodybuilders sport well–defined muscles and aerobicizers small waistlines. Cyclists and runners possess incredible endurance. People who emphasize flexibility can squeeze into glass boxes. Nobody likes to stretch except Baryshnikov. A stretching program improves your posture and grace. Walkers and runners can stretch to improve their performance. Stretching is a relaxing method of mental preparation prior to training.

Make Time to Stretch

Flexibility exercises take only a few minutes and require no special equipment other than loose clothing. Sometimes I stretch in front of the TV. When my kids see me stretching they jump on my back, forcing me into a deeper pose. My two year old daughter mimics my Chinese splits and raises her leg effortlessly to her forehead. I always stretch after running, weight–training, and after my last workout of the day.

Stretching Prevents Injury

Have you pulled a muscle sprinting to first base and wished you had stretched? Warm up, then stretch. If you don't believe me, pull a piece of steak out of the freezer and try to bend it. It snaps – the same way your cold muscle might. Years ago people did cold ballistic stretches and wondered why they pulled muscles. Up and down they bounced, moaning and groaning. Static stretching maintains your joints and prevents low back and other spinal column problems.

Stretch Slow

A slow, continuous stretch is desired. Exhale as you move into each position. Hold for twenty seconds. Slowly stretch to the limits of joint motion until you feel tension in your muscle. Then relax. Go for comfort. Soft music in the background is nice. Stretch without a teeth–clenching, red–ballooned face. Monitor your joints, muscles, and tendons. Perform an inventory of your body. No pain is gain. Settle into your pose like a yogi. Your body will adapt and soon you will stretch comfortably. Learn to hold your stretch for at least twenty seconds to fully relax the muscle. This will allow for a greater and more comfortable stretch. Within months you may stretch to a slight level of discomfort but never approaching pain.

Stretch Gracefully

A multitude of variables will affect your flexibility. On warm days you are a rubber band while on cooler days you're a doggy knot. You can elongate muscles more comfortably in the afternoon than in the morning. Perform your routine with the grace and control of Jean Claude Van Damme limbering up for a fight scene. A millimeter of increased flexibility is similar to a ten miles per hour increase in your serve.

No Competition

Most girls can stretch farther than guys. Don't compare yourself to an ex–cheerleader who jumps into a full split. Nevertheless, males who begin stretching at a young age can maintain a high degree of flexibility. I started stretching when I was thirteen. Twenty–five years later I am more Gumby–like than when I was a youngster. I haven't missed two days of stretching since. It is unnecessary to stretch every day, but I feel stiff if I miss. My motivation for stretching comes from observing stooped–over, decrepit, crotchety folks compared with sixty–year–old Tiger Kim, who jumped up, broke a board, then landed gracefully into a full split.

Stretching Improves Muscle

Stretching helps your cross–training. Research suggests that stretching can split muscle fibers and increase their number. More importantly stretching gives muscles a longer range of movement, allowing for a fuller extension and contraction. Fitness expert John Parillo claims that by stretching the fascia, the muscle has more room to grow.

Stretching Relaxes the Mind

The suppleness of your body will affect the flexibility of your mind. Stretching loosens your mind. You can become an expert on your personal flexibility program, and your movements will become second nature. Without thinking about your movements, you can mentally prepare for your impending workout or performance.

Stretching Feels Good

Be sure to stretch the antagonist of your major muscle groups. The antagonist to the biceps is the triceps. The antagonist to the quadriceps is the hamstrings. The more flexible you are the better cross–trainer you will be. You can reach for a ball more easily, and you can crouch into a lower defensive position. Stretching alleviates delayed onset muscle soreness (DOMS) because it may relax potential muscle spasms. Stretching the quadriceps, hamstrings, and hips helps protect the knee and lower spine from injury.

Stretch Antagonists

A minimum amount of flexibility is required to realize gains in your cross–training program. If you have poor flexibility, you will gain strength at a slower rate than someone who has moderate flexibility. If your hamstrings are extremely tight, you will find it difficult to gain optimum strength in your quadriceps. The muscle spindles in your hamstrings shut down your quadriceps during the final stages of your exercise if your hamstrings are tight. Parillo goes on to say that between the muscles and the tendons there is a group of sensory receptors called the golgi tendon organ which fire during high intensity workouts, shutting the muscle down to prevent injury.

Active Isolate (A–I) Stretching

A–I is becoming increasingly popular for cross–trainers across the country. First, flex the antagonist muscle opposite the muscle you want to stretch. After you have contracted the opposing muscle fully, gently stretch the antagonist muscle until you feel slight tension. Hold for two seconds. Then relax. In an A–I biceps stretch, you flex your triceps for two seconds before you stretch your biceps for two seconds, which forces the biceps to relax automatically. Then you alternate flexing the triceps andstretching the biceps for eight repetitions. You can do A–I for every antagonist muscle group in the body (ie. quadriceps–hamstring, etc.).

A–I Side Leg Stretch

Your supporting foot remains flat while you extend your other leg to the side. Flex the quadriceps of your extended leg. Hold for three seconds and then stretch until you feel tension in the inner thigh of your extended leg. Hold the stretch for three seconds. Repeat with the other leg.

A–I Side Split

Spread your legs out as far as possible. Flex your quadriceps for three seconds. Let your body weight push you down until you feel tension in your inner thighs. Hold at tension for thirty seconds.

A–I Front Split, Chest to Floor

Perform the side split. Lift your toes up toward the ceiling. Flex your quadriceps for three seconds and then slowly bring your chest toward the floor. When you feel tension, hold for thirty seconds.

A–I Front Split, Forehead to Shin

Sit in a front split. Flex the quadriceps on your front leg and pull your chest toward your knee, and your forehead toward your shin. Keep your back flat. When you feel tension, hold for three seconds. Repeat with the other side.

A–I Forehead to Toes

Sit with your back flat and the bottoms of your feet together. Pull your feet in as close to your groin as possible. Flex your quadriceps for three seconds and then grab your toes. Slowly bring your chest toward your toes.

A–I Butterfly

From the forehead to toes position, flex your quadriceps for three seconds and grab your ankles and push your knees toward the floor with your elbows.

A–I Quadriceps Stretch

Extend your left leg out to the front. Bend your right leg at a ninety degree angle with your right foot adjacent to your hip. Lie back and slowly attempt to lower your right knee toward the floor. Be careful not to put too much pressure on the inside of the knee. Flex the muscles in your right hamstring and hold for three seconds. Then relax until you feel tension from the stretch in your right quadriceps. Switch legs and repeat the exercise.

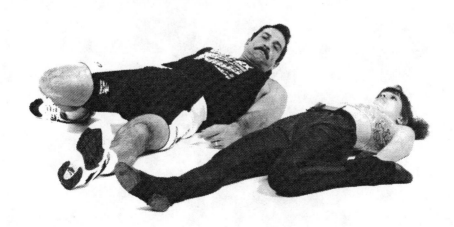

PNF

Stretching by yourself is fantastic, but proprioceptive neuromuscular facilitation (PNF) will provide mega–results. Your partner pulls you slowly into a perfect stretch. When you feel tension, you relax and allow your partner to pull just a tad more. My students improved one hundred percent in sixteen weeks doing PNF twice a week. A partner helps them achieve a greater stretch than they dreamed possible. Be easy on your partner. Stretch your partner to the point of tension, hold, and then relax. The same warm–up rules apply to PNF as solo stretching.

PNF Hamstring Wall Stretch

Stand with your back and heels flat against a wall with both knees slightly bent. Let your partner grab your right ankle and slowly lift it until you feel tension. When you feel tension, tell your partner to stop. Pull from your right hamstring and press the back of your heel toward the floor while your partner resists for three seconds. Relax and repeat with your left leg.

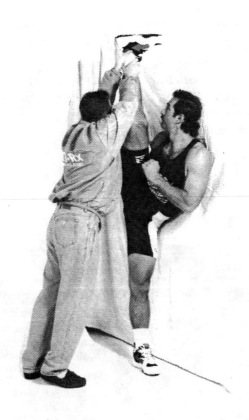

PNF Inner Thigh Stretch

Stand sideways to the wall with both knees slightly bent. Let your partner grab your right ankle and slowly lift it until you feel tension. Be sure your toes point sideways through the duration. When you feel tension, tell your partner to stop. Pull from your right inner thigh back toward the floor while your partner resists for three seconds. Relax and repeat with your left leg.

PNF Hip Stretch

Stand facing the wall with both knees slightly bent. Place your hands comfortably on the wall for balance. Let your partner grab your right ankle and slowly lift it until you feel tension. Be sure the toes on your right foot point down. When you feel tension tell your partner to stop. Pull from your hip toward the floor while your partner resists for three seconds. Relax and repeat with your left leg.

POSTURE

Perfect Posture

Stretching is important, but good posture is a necessity. For every inch your head is held in front of your shoulders, you are placing fifteen pounds of extra strain on your neck according to posture expert Carole Lewis, Ph.D. Good posture helps you to add inches to your height, flatten your tummy, and avoid lower back pain. Poor posture draws the shoulders forward, collapsing the chest, decreasing oxygen transfer to the muscles and the brain, says sports medicine specialist Jenny Stone. Weight training and stretching will help, but developing good posture takes time. Muscles must be retrained to feel comfortable in their new position.

Back in Shape

Eight out of ten Americans will eventually suffer from back pain. To prevent a "bad back", strengthen your abdominals, hips, and legs, and stretch your hamstrings. Flexible hamstrings and strong supporting muscles will help to maintain proper pelvic alignment and perfect posture.

(To chart your flexibility see Chart F on page 89.)

Running and Stretching Rules and Regulations

1. Your running and stretching routine should be easy. If you don't love it, you won't do it.

2. Running and stretching works! Run and stretch at least three times per week.

3. It's O.K. to do aerobics every day. You may vary the activity.

4. If running bothers your ankles, ride a bike. If riding a bike hurts your knees, try stair climbing.

5. Avoid running with your significant other, unless you promise not to act like a big shot.

6. Incorporate stretching into your running regimen to gain flexibility.

7. Alternate hard and easy days if you cross–train similar activities such as jogging and walking.

8. Cross–train to gain without the pain.

9. Cross–train before work to make sure you get it in.

10. Cross–train with people or alone for a change of pace.

11. Develop an indoor cross–training program in case of inclement weather.

12. Think about a cross–training routine when you travel.

13. If you're short on time, cross–train in small increments throughout the day.

14. Regular endurance exercise without strength training does not prevent muscle loss.

Chart

FLEXIBILITY

	Date	Time	Intensity	Feelings
Side Leg Stretch				
Side Split				
Chest to Floor				
Forehead to Shin				
Forehead to Toes				
Butterfly				
Lower Back Stretch				
Shoulder Stretch				
Quadriceps Stretch				

RUNNING

Start Easy

Misplaced Aspirations

I wanted to be a cross–trainer since I was thirteen years old. My passions were karate and tennis, and in high school I tried out for the cross–country team. No one told me I was supposed to be running over the summer. The first practice was a twelve–mile run. I finished the twelve miles, remained in bed for the rest of that day and the next. My first day was my last day on the cross–country team.

If you are beginning a fitness program, walk before you jog. Walking for thirty minutes will prepare your muscles for jogging. When you can walk continuously for thirty minutes, you are ready to jog. On your first walk–jog workout, walk for seven minutes and then jog for three. Jog at a fast walking pace. Repeat this three times for a total of thirty minutes. When you feel ready, walk for five minutes and then jog for five. In a few months you may be able to jog the entire thirty minutes.

Jogging and Running

Jog in an upright position, stomach in, heel to toe, taking short, smooth strides. Pick up your feet, lifting your front knee and extending your back leg. Keep your elbows bent, your forearms and chin parallel to the ground. Breathe deeply from your diaphragm. Smile. Pretend you love it. Some people measure their heart rate at intervals throughout their workout, others wear heart–rate monitors. Jogging three to five times a week at eighty percent of your maximum speed is enough to reach a high level of cardiovascular fitness. If you feel winded, look around. If no one is watching, slow to a walk. Don't ignore discomfort in your shins, knees, or back. Pay attention to your body.

Anyone Can Run

I played collegiate tennis at Penn State. After I lost a match (I lost most of my matches), the coach could never find me. Instead of watching the rest of the team lose, I drowned my sorrow by cross–training with weights and a rejuvenating five–mile run. Running loosened my muscles and my mind. I wasn't fast or efficient; but by the time I returned, I felt like a winner.

Running Increases Endurance

After college I was fortunate to make the United States Taekwondo Team. At two hundred pounds I was not the most agile competitor. I waited for my opponents to get tired and surprised them by landing winning kicks.

Competition is My Excuse to Train

The best parts were the workouts. At the Olympic Training Center we cross–trained running bleachers and wind–sprints. We traveled to Taiwan for the pre–World Taekwondo Games. While my teammates grudgingly sat on guided bus tours, I enjoyed jogging the streets of Taipei, experiencing the real China.

Truth Serum

Between taekwondo tournaments, I was accepted to a graduate program in sports psychology. Many of my professors were cross–trainers. Running loosened our tongues. Jogging around the golf course took the coat and tie off my most serious instructors.

Gender Differences

My statistics professor convinced me to enter a ten kilometer race. I stood anxiously near the front of the pack awaiting the starting gun. I recognized Olympian Francie Larrieu Smith and decided I could keep up with her because she was female. She took off like a gazelle, but I knew I could hang on because I was a man and men are stronger. As the race progressed, I grew mesmerized by Francie's effortless stride. I remained two feet behind her until the four mile mark when she cranked up a hill, leaving me in her dust. I finished in thirty–nine minutes and loped over to my buddy Jimmy Smith to brag about my time. When I asked how Francie did, he said she heard some old man wheezing behind her for half the race and finally took off.

Balance Your Program

Running Faster

According to Owen Anderson, Ph.D., you can run faster by speeding up your stride. Twenty percent of runners "overstride" and produce a "braking" effect, decreasing running efficiency. Exercise physiologist Jack Daniels, Ph.D., found that the best stride rate for most distance runners is ninety strides per minute. To increase your speed, count your steps as you run. Gradually increase your steps to a maximum of ninety per minute. At first your stride length will decrease. To normalize it, run hills. Hill training strengthens your legs which helps you regain your stride length. Taking quicker steps will force you to apply more force to the ground more quickly, thereby increasing your speed.

Running Enhances Health

Dr. Walter Bortz of Stanford Medical School described running as an option for young people; but for older people, it's a must. His article in Fortune magazine profiled an eight year study comparing five hundred runners vs. non-runners aged fifty and over. In the beginning runners had a two–to–one advantage over non–runners in a variety of health measures. After eight years, there was a five–to–one advantage for the runners.

Cross-Training and Running

The lessons I learned from running have been fascinating. I continued running when I was hired for my first job in Houston, Texas. I jogged with my students, sometimes carrying six pound dumbells to raise my heart rate. If you pump your arms while holding weights, your heart rate will skyrocket. Hold your weights with a soft grip and be sure to progress gradually.

Doug Lentz, director of Chambersburg Physical Therapy, reminds us that running improves the lungs and heart but may result in muscle imbalances. Running stresses the back of the leg but does little for the front leg muscles and upper body. Owen Anderson presented some recent research suggesting cross-training with weights strengthens the legs to keep them balanced. He said strength training increases fast–twitch muscle fiber in much the same way that sprinting does. David Costill, Ph.D., director of Ball State University's Human Performance Laboratory, agrees that weight training may substitute for speed work, minimizing the risk of injury. There aren't the jarring forces with weight training, according to Costill. Work each of the major muscle groups in the legs including quadriceps, hamstrings, gluteus maximus, and calves. Upper–body resistance cross–training allows one to run faster and further. If the upper body fatigues, a runner expends more energy and actually slows. Once fast–twitch fibers are gone, they're gone for good. Don't allow them to atrophy says Costill.

Cycling

Another way to strengthen the legs is to cross–train with cycling. Joan Benoit Samuelson had a debilitating knee injury but trained furiously on a stationary bike and won a gold medal in the Olympic marathon. Frank Shorter, another Olympic marathoner, extolled the benefits of cycling. Other studies demonstrate that runners who cross–trained with cycling improved their quadriceps strength by twenty percent in only four weeks. A runner can use cycling to rehabilitate an injury and maintain performance for as long as six weeks. Pedaling is also a good cool–down. A University of Northern Iowa study demonstrated that pedaling a stationary bicycle at forty percent of maximum oxygen consumption removed more lactic acid from the muscles faster than massage or passive recovery.

Ergogenic Aids

Special carbohydrate–loading liquids and energy bars lead the list of ergogenic aids. Marathoners routinely sip sports drinks and choke down energy bars while on the run. Some believe creatine monohydrate aids endurance while others rely on caffeine. Sniffing peppermint, menthol, or eucalyptus can energize you according to studies at Duke University.

Fad Diets

There are a variety of untested theories. Twenty year old world ten thousand meter record holder Wang Junxia of China scarfs down a diet of worms, caterpillar fungus, and a soup made of turtle blood. Wang's coach has sold this elixir to aspiring runners and made over one million dollars.

Aging Gracefully

My alarm clock signals my first workout of the day. I stumble out the door before dawn so my lack of speed and purposeless stride are invisible to all but the paper boy. My run lasts for little more than twenty minutes, but it warms me up for stretching.

(To chart your walking/running progress see Chart G on page 95.)

Chart

WALKING/RUNNING

Date	Time	Duration	Intensity	Mileage	Feelings

8

ONE MORE REP!
ONE MORE LAP!

Spinning Your Wheels

Fred cross–trains three times a week but never gets fitter. He strolls in the gym, does multiple sets and repetitions, walks every other day, but hardly breaks a sweat. He appears to be getting a workout, but months and years go by without improvement.

Intensity

Unlike Fred, most of us realize that the first few moments of cross–training mean little. To put on slabs of muscle, enhance aerobic capacity, and improve flexibility, it's the last few minutes that count. A former bodybuilding Mr. Universe goes a step further saying you need only do one set per body part per week, training to failure on each set to maximize hypertrophy (muscle size). Similarly, champion endurance athletes contend it's not the quantity of mileage but the quality.

Cycle Your Training

Imagine the horror of cross–training to failure each session, month after month, year after year. It's no wonder sixty–one percent of those who begin a workout program quit within the first four weeks. To grow muscle, enhance aerobics, or increase flexibility without losing motivation, there is a middle road. You can trick your body to enjoy pain. Mix it up. Cycle your cross–training. A light day now and then can be beneficial.

No Pain No Gain

When cross–training becomes uncomfortable, you stop. But if you never take the opportunity to endure, you miss out. Relax. Get used to it. Pain makes you better. Face discomfort. Learn about it, and cross–training won't seem severe. Accept pain for what it is and handle it. Without pain, there is no accomplishment or real happiness. Pain is uncomfortable, but it's not the end of the world. Some respond to pain with anger and hostility, but research demonstrates these responses increase stress. Cross–training is not just physical. Learn to respond to cross–training pain with acceptance. William James noted that humans have the power to change their inner minds which ultimately changes their lives.

Your Brain Controls Pain

Pain is a multifaceted phenomena that is part of everyone's life. Pain is natural and positive, albeit potentially uncomfortable. The origin of cross–training pain is not at issue, controlling it is. We will not discuss "bad" pain – muscle tears or broken bones – but the pain of intense training that stops when you stop.

Lactic Acid Pain

Human nature is to avoid pain when it occurs. But if you never challenge it, you miss out on the ecstasy of pushing the physical limitations of the human machine. Change how you think about pain. The burning in your muscles during strenuous exercise is caused by lactic acid. Muscles generate lactic acid for the duration of your cross–training effort, but the kidneys and liver absorb it. Exercise physiologist David Swain suggests that the bloodstream is like a bank. There are lactic acid deposits and lactic acid withdrawals, but the lactic acid level remains relatively constant. When you reach your anaerobic threshold (AT), however, the lactic acid production exceeds the removal rate; and the acid remains in the muscles, causing pain.

Depleted Endorphins

The body deals with conflicting sensations of pain in different ways. I was riding my bike down an old country road when, without warning, a black blur streaked in front of me. I shouted in surprise as I broad–sided a Labrador retriever. He swept the front wheel out from under me, and I landed on my head. Blood streamed down my neck, but I felt nothing. I straightened my front wheel and continued to ride. By the time I arrived home, lactic acid settled in my muscles and my endorphins were depleted.

Competing Pain Signals

Receptors transmitted pain to my brain at the scene of the accident and during my ride home, but there were other signals as well. Burning quadriceps and labored breathing drowned out the stinging in my scalp. At home, however, there was no stimulation to compete with my throbbing head and road–rash, so a new pain took center stage. According to Melzack's Gate Control Theory, a popular hypothesis on the workings of pain, thousands of pain signals come together across nerve fibers that meet between the spinal cord and the brain. This traffic jam of signals allows some signals to get through while others wait; some never make it.

Playing in Pain

Pain can be mysteriously overridden. Pavlov administered an electric shock to a dog's paw and rewarded the animal with food. In a short time, following each shock, the dog's whines and struggles changed to salivation and tail–wagging. Harvard scientists gave morphine to one group of patients after surgery and placebos (sugar pills) to another group. Seventy five percent of the placebo group felt the same relief as if they had taken the morphine. Professional athletes play injured for millions of dollars. A hypnotized subject does not feel a pin–prick. In the Amazon Valley an expectant mother spends three hours in seemingly pain–free labor, then returns to work after giving birth. Every culture has its own traditions and incentives.

My Pain is Not Your Pain

Nerves send pain messages to the spinal cord which delivers them to the brain. Sean McCann, sport psychologist at the Olympic Training Center, teaches athletes to use key words and imagery to reinterpret pain signals more positively. Pain diminishes when you call it something else. Simonton, M.D., says to picture your lactic acid pain as a glowing orange ball. Then see your body fending off the pain (for example the lactic acid glowing orange ball disappearing). A person may describe pain as sharp, dull, chronic, or overpowering; but another will never truly understand the description. McCann suggests "Don't say the pain will be over soon." You're surrendering. Learn and practice the art of association. Focus exclusively on your effort. You must be in control of your pain.

Augmenters or Reducers

According to psychologist Jerry Parker, what you think and feel affects the experience of pain. He says pain is sensory, emotional, and cognitive. The pain messages that reach the brain may be controlled. The mind can magnify pain or sublimate it. Pain signals scream so loudly they drown out rational thought. Change those howls of agony to shouts of joy. The first few days of a serious cross–training schedule are the most intense. Muscle fibers split and joints ache. You can choose to interpret these signals as debilitating or change them to wonderful sensations of cross–training success. PREPARATION: Your ability to handle pain is what sets you apart from the also–rans and the couch potatoes. Approach cross–training pain with courage. Deal with it on your terms. Handle pain one step at a time. Preparation for pain helps cross–trainers endure it. Modern triathletes, bodybuilders, and ultra–endurance athletes revel in pain. That last repetition may seem severe, but the brain transforms it into joy.

Rock–N–Roll Pain Killer

Psychologists claim humans need some pain in order to function. We seek an optimum level of pain—a level we can handle. Goal–directed pain may be endured. When I broke the twenty–four hour cycling distance record, I experienced pain the entire ride. Rather than succumb, I acknowledged pain's presence and focused on a rock–n–roll tape. Rock–n–roll was my cross–training pain killer. The lactic acid burn of a cross–training workout is a joy, especially when it is over.

Pain Protects

Pain is an "in the moment" experience. Try reading this sentence with your finger hovering over a flame and see which gets your attention. Pain protects cross–trainers from injury. While experiencing the doldrums of the Race Across America, I promised I would never attempt it again. A week after completing the race however, I was training for the next year's event. Similarly, the pain of childbirth is sometimes forgotten when the mother finds out she is unexpectedly pregnant again.

Laughter and Pain

Studies have shown that laughter significantly affects a person's ability to handle pain. The relaxation following laughter alleviates agonizing muscle spasms. Cancer patient Norman Cousins made the joyous discovery that ten minutes of belly laughter had an anesthetic effect and gave him two hours of pain–free sleep. He believed watching hours of funny movies helped drive his cancer into remission. Researchers claim ten minutes of laughter is equivalent to a thirty minute jog. Laughter increases your breathing, thereby increasing the amount of oxygen in the blood, according to the April, 1994 issue of the Journal of the American Medical Association. It increases circulation and delivery of nutrients throughout the body and helps clear mucus from the lungs.

Dissociation

Dissociation is setting the mind apart from the body. A recent study by David Roth, Ph.D., on one hundred fifty recreational runners demonstrated that dissociation provided them with more vigor both during and after their run. The top eight dissociation topics included relationships, housework, building homes, life problems, natural surroundings, job and career, recent hurt or anger, and finances. Any cross–training endeavor requires a certain amount of boredom and discomfort. Plenty of world–class athletes and entertainers dissociate from the boredom and pain of their training and performance. A fire–walker's feet are burning over hot coals, but his attention is elsewhere. Houdini distanced himself from pain to escape strait jackets. Dissociation allows you to sit still for a three–hour movie. When dissociated, you can drive hundreds of miles in a seemingly few minutes. Changing your mind about discomfort can change your body.

(To monitor your pain management skills see Chart H on page 105.)

Endorphins

Are you pushing the outside of your cross–training envelope? Search yourself for the reason you love to train. Some reach an "endorphin high" during their training. Endorphins are a morphine–like substance that attaches to nerve cell receptors in the brain. The receptors combine with the chemicals blocking the transmission of pain. A feeling of joy is the result. The so–called endorphin release has also been shown to alleviate depression. Research by a foremost authority on endorphins, Atko Vuru, Ph.D., shows that to experience endorphins you must exercise at seventy–six percent of your maximum heart rate. Some people experience the "endorphin high" in thirty minutes. For others it may take as long as two hours or more and ten percent of the population never feel it.

Enjoy Your Endorphins

Recent research by University of Richmond exercise physiologists suggests exercise that is familiar may produce more pain–reducing endorphins than exercise that isn't. Dr. Owen Anderson's explanation is that although the workouts felt equally strenuous, the one they were accustomed to was likely to produce the increased work and greater endorphin release. However, Lee Berk, Ph.D., showed that endorphins can be produced simply by anticipating activity.

Sport Psychology

Most athletes agree that at least fifty percent of their sport is mental. But how much time do they spend in mental preparation? Each evening as a sport psychology researcher, my duties included performing experiments on human subjects. I lured unsuspecting college students to the sport psychology lab. In the first experiment I competed with subjects on an isokinetic leg strength machine. Half of the subjects were told I was a world class athlete, and I demonstrated such by exploding the needle off the screen, easily beating each subject (I cheated). The other half were told I had a leg injury and wouldn't perform well (I faked a weak attempt). Then each subject and I competed in a muscular endurance task from a seated position, extending our right leg and holding it above a string. If either of us touched the string with our foot, the light went off signaling a loss. I surreptitiously slipped a ball under my thigh for support. The subjects who beat me on the isokinetic leg strength machine grunted and sweated their way to exemplary performances, holding their legs up significantly longer than those who expected to lose to a world class athlete.

Expectations

Ness and Patton published another study that demonstrated the power of expectations on strength performance. A subject failed at a three hundred pound bench press, but he benched two hundred ninety–five pounds regularly. Unbeknownst to the subject, the experimenter–coach added a two and one–half pound plate to each side of the two hundred ninety–five pound bar. Afterwards he and his coach celebrated his three hundred pound lift.

The effect of expectation on performance was apparent during my first twenty–four hour cycling race. No one told me how far I had ridden until the final moments of the race. I had set a new record by fifty–eight miles! During the final hours of the race, each pedal stroke was painful. Had I known I had broken the record I probably would have slowed. Since then I have failed to endure the pain necessary to set a new record.

Audience Arousal

Expectations can dramatically affect your ability to get through the pain. So can an audience. Sport psychologists call this phenomenon social facilitation. The mere presence of someone in the room can excite you through discomfort to reach your goal, especially if that someone is an evaluator or significant other.

Stimulants

Other aids athletes use are caffeine, ephedrine, and a variety of other stimulants. A natural, healthy method is termed "preparatory arousal." In our preparatory arousal study I asked each subject to test his leg strength on the isokinetic leg extension machine. Thirty seconds before performing a one repetition maximum, I asked each subject to do one of the following:

A. Association

Concentrate on the upcoming task. Concentration in weight training requires a narrow–internal focus of attention, as opposed to the broad–external focus a football quarterback must possess. You can choose to associate with the lift by "feeling" every aspect of the range of motion. You visualize fibers splitting and blood pumping to finish out his repetitions.

B. Self-Talk

Talk to yourself about the upcoming task. Power lifters yell and scream at themselves to get their repetition. Self–talk takes the form of positive affirmations such as "I can do it." These self–verbalizations raise arousal levels.

C. Relaxation

Relax all the muscles in your body. Relaxation training can help a bodybuilder notice if unnecessary muscle fibers are used during the workout. For example, if you are trying to isolate your back but you pull from your biceps instead of your elbows, tension in your arms undermines your progress.

D. Imagery

Picture yourself doing the task. Imagery is a tool that bodybuilders use to enhance their physiques. Several studies by Suinn and Hale suggest that when one visualizes completing an exercise, nervous impulses are sent down the proper neuromuscular pathways to stimulate muscle fibers to lift the weight.

E. Preparatory Arousal

Get psyched and explode on the machine. Preparatory arousal allows the individual to get pumped, psyched, wired. You can do anything to pump yourself up.

Mental Preparation Works

The preparatory arousal group (E) performed significantly better than the other four groups. Since then, however, further research has demonstrated that an individualized approach to association, self–talk, relaxation, and imagery all play major roles in improving cross–training performance.

Comments

1. Set attainable cross–training goals.

2. Visualize yourself completing your repetitions or laps.

3. Dissociate on the first phase of your training and associate on your final phase.

4. Teach your body to handle discomfort a little at a time.

5. Reach deep inside and ask a little more of yourself each workout.

6. Practice preparatory arousal, imagery, association, and self–talk strategies regularly.

7. Expect to get through discomfort.

8. Have a friend watch you.

CROSS-TRAINING

PAIN MANAGEMENT

Mode of Exercise	Date	Time	Intensity	Duration	Feelings

MUSCLE
and
ENDURANCE

Goals

Most assume it impossible to win endurance contests and have a chiseled muscular look. Experts claim muscle–heads and elite aerobicizers are mutually exclusive because high intensity aerobics eats up muscle tissue while lugging extra meat around the track is inefficient for endurance performance. Exercise scientist Don Chu claims that the body adapts to the demands of your workout. If you do a lot of aerobics, your body will mold itself into the shape of a sinewy marathoner. Marathoners struggle to pick up a suitcase, and power lifters get winded climbing a flight of stairs.

Fuel

There is evidence, however, that if you eat right, lift weights, and rest between bouts of aerobics, you can cross–train into a lean, muscular, endurance animal. You must eat additional carbohydrates and protein to fuel, grow, and repair your muscles. If you do not, you may feel sluggish and your body may use the protein from your muscle for energy.

Planning

Plan your cross–training goals. Cardiologist Paul Thompson points out that if you do not exercise, you lose endurance and strength as you grow older. Sitting around can cause you to lose ten percent of your cardiovascular ability per decade after age thirty. Your heart and lungs lose their efficiency in forty-eight to seventy-two hours.

Impact sports such as running can break down your muscle. That's one reason top–notch marathoners show little significant muscle in their upper bodies. To retain muscle, choose an anti–catabolic low–impact endurance activity. Cross–train your weight–lifting program with walking, cycling, in–line skating, or low–impact aerobic dance. Smooth movements do not tear down as much muscle as pounding the pavement. Cross–train your workouts into several sessions spersed throughout the day with feedings. I lift weights before breakfast, do two hours of cycling before lunch, and two more hours before dinner.

Weights Work

Follow a resistance program that fits your lifestyle. If you are aerobicizing every day, weight training in the morning works best. To get in and out of the gym, train one or two body parts per workout on a split routine.

Cross–Training Split Routine

Day 1:   Cross–train your chest with your frontal deltoids and abdominals.

Day 2:   Cross–train your back with your lateral deltoids and trapezius.

Day 3:   Cross–train your legs* with your forearms.

Day 4:   Rest day.

Day 5:   Begin your program again.

---

*Your legs may not improve at the same rate as your upper body because your legs may be chronically overtrained from aerobics. Train your legs on aerobic rest days.

Muscle Power

Weight training can increase your fast–twitch type II fibers and strengthen the muscles surrounding your joints, protecting them from injury and improving strength. Increased muscle translates into improved strength, potentially enhancing your anaerobic threshold, speed, power, and overall performance.

Aerobics

Aerobicizers in the 1980's blindly chanted through repetitions of tummy-toners and thigh–slimmers. Students prayed away fat, glancing longingly at the clock. Minutes ticked slowly by. For some it was the longest hour of their lives, huffing and puffing while feigning grace and balance. A strain here, a muscle pull there, they tried to keep up.

Aerobics Now

Aerobics in the 1990's is different. Some emphasize yoga stretches; others punch and kick to music. Many use step–programs on benches, and a few do low–impact lateral slides. Most spend time cooling down with meditation, centering, or prayer. Although researchers recommend thirty minutes of aerobics persession, the *1990 American Journal of Cardiology* indicated that three ten–minute exercise sessions per day at seventy percent of maximum heart rate had similar cardiovascular benefits. A more recent Stanford study demonstrated that when subjects pedaled a stationary bicycle for short periods through the day, they had the same benefits as those who rode non–stop for half an hour.

Benefits of Aerobics

1. Increases mitochondria and capillary density which results in more blood vessels delivering more oxygen to muscles.

2. Improved oxygen uptake and decreased resting heart rate, blood pressure, and blood–fat levels.

3. Increased ability to use fat to fuel your activity.

4. Increased total amount of blood pumped to the muscles. Withincreased blood flow, blood toxins are removed more efficiently so you can rest less between sets, recover quicker, and strengthen your heart and blood vessels.

5. Increased energy systems of your entire body.

6. Increased anaerobic threshold and cardiovascular function may carry over into your other activities, allowing you to perform more efficiently and intensely.

7. Increased ability to switch effectively from anaerobics to endurance activities such as from weight training to running.

8. Decreased blood pressure. Blood vessels become wider and more profuse allowing reduced pressure in the artery andcapillary walls.

Cross-Training Aerobics

Form, breathing, and posture are emphasized. There is a warm–up, stretching, toning, dumbells, aerobic, plyometric, and cool–down stretch program. But there is no counting repetitions. Aerobicizers train by themselves, with partners, or in groups. Students are not concerned about keeping up; they pace themselves. Nobody is frantically taking heart rates; cross–trainers monitor their perceived exertion. The jargon is different, positive vibes are apparent, and there are fewer dropouts. Studies demonstrate that a key to exercise adherence is variety. Constant diversity develops ultimate fitness without overtraining a certain part of the body. A heavy-set jogger may save his knees by cross-training with swimming.

Partners

Cross–training partners are more than partners. They initiate conversation. They fill in the gaps when their buddies are busy breathing. Jokes and sarcasm are okay. Fun is part of the workout. Everyone joins in. If an aerobicizer is down, the partner provides support. Cross–training aerobics is an exercise encounter–session, and the partner is the facilitator. They share stories, anecdotes, wise–cracks, and tragedies. Some give advice about car repair, medical problems, and stock options. Dr. Michael Sachs from the University of Maryland stated that social relationships can be important in improving an individual's participation in an activity, increasing the probability of adherence.

Groups

Cross–training aerobicizers enjoy the benefits of group dynamics. Sport psychologist Robert Zajonc's social facilitation theory predicts that an audience increases arousal and excitement. Partners, or members of cross–training aerobics, serve as their own audience. If an aerobicizer has mastered a bench routine, an increase in arousal will benefit performance. However, a pumped–up novice may trip, fall, or suffer a knee injury because of audience–aroused overexertion.

Flow

Cross–training aerobicizers flow. Csikszentmihalyi coined the term flow and defined it as a feeling of control without ego. Tennis guru Jim Loehr describes flow as being in the zone. Some physiologists refer to it as an endorphin effect. Sport psychologist William Morgan calls the well–being a person feels during and after exercise the "feel–better phenomenon." Cross–training aerobicizers cultivate a peak experience in every workout. The physical routine is aligned to the potential and goals of each cross–trainer. If an aerobicizer injured her back, she may perform weighted leg curls while her comrade is doing bent–leg–deadlifts.

Solitary Aerobics

Cross–trainers demand a gradual progression and an easy–to–follow sequence of movements. They free their minds from their bodies. Their routine is second nature. Cycling, swimming, jumping rope, racket sports against a wall,treadmill, stairmaster, stationary bike, cross–country ski machine, jogging, aqua–aerobics, hitting a punching bag, karate, dance, aerobic–golf, aerobic–basketball, backpacking, fitness–walking, and in–line skating are a few cross–training aerobic choices.

Individualized Training

Cross–training aerobicizers are on different health, fitness, and athletic programs. Newcomers to cross–training may try to shed thirty pounds. Intermediates attempt to tone flabby muscles. Advanced aspire to be better athletes. Cross–training beginners relax and enjoy their routine while advanced cross–trainers perform more repetitions and faster movements. At the University of Western

Ontario–Canada, eight men exercised three days a week for twenty–four weeks at eighty–five percent of their maximum heart rate. They improved their steady state aerobic conditioning by fifty percent.

Quality

Budgeting time for aerobics is difficult. I spend over thirty hours a week on my bike, stairmaster, and stationary bicycle. But I'm training for the Race Across America. My program is not your program. You may decide to cross–train for a sixty kilometer bike tour or a ten kilometer run. The quality of your training is more important than the quantity. Pay attention to your body, and allow time for recovery.

Balance

When schedules get busy, people often quit cross–training rather than cut back a little. If you neglect any aspect of your cross–training, it will be noticed. Taking a week off is okay; but if you take a month off, you will lose a tremendous part of your fitness. Eating high–fat and sugary foods and foregoing your weight training and aerobics for a month may set you back three months. Increased mitochondria and muscle require more calories, so you must consume more quality food. If time is at a premium, you can retain your conditioning by maintaining your intensity. Instead of training each body part twice a week on the weights, work each body part high intensity once a week. If you previously rode your bike six days a week, cut down to three fast rides.

You Can

Nobody thought it possible to maintain slabs of muscle while cross–training a high–intensity endurance program, but you can. Aerobic training changes your muscle chemistry so you can use oxygen more efficiently. Capillaries increase for better oxygen dispersal which enables the heart to pump more blood to muscles and tissue. As you fall asleep, imagine your world–class heart and lungs pumping oxygen to your powerful muscles.

1. **On a budget:** Run, jog, walk, jump rope, swim in a lake, lift weights at a high school, college, or recreation center.

2. **No time:** Set your alarm thirty minutes early for a before–work workout. Eat lunch in ten minutes and walk for twenty. Before you walk in your front door for your evening binge, walk around the block.

3. **No interest:** Get a partner. Try headphones. Set a different goal. Read fitness magazines. Try a new sport. Do a family member's workout.

(To monitor your cardiovascular progress see Your Cardiovascular Choice Chart I on page 113.)

Chart

YOUR CARDIOVASCULAR CHOICE

Date	Time	Intensity	Duration	Mileage	Feelings

10

LESS is BEST -ATTITUDE

Scheduling

Get up, shower, eat breakfast, go to work, work out, come home, eat dinner, watch television, go to bed. Same ol' same ol.' A rut can be pleasant and satisfying, if you're an old geezer. Consider the quiet and measured daily rituals of a monk. A disciplined ritualistic monastic life is good for some but not for me. Meditation doesn't pay the bills. It is difficult to break patterns. And order is comfortable. But if you're stale and bored, then it's cross–training time!

Rest

Prevent over–training by scheduling rest periods and sleep. Restful activities may include reading, writing, television, eating, sleeping, and family time. According to Buskin and Goldring's research some Americans relax by taking baths, calling friends, and going shopping. There is a push–pull, yin–yang, give–and–take that assures balance in any cross–training program. Activity is cross–trained with relaxation. A twenty minute mid–day recovery cycle between workouts may energize cross–trainers for peak performance. Beware. A break exceeding 20 minutes leaves cross–trainers sleeping on the couch. Billie Jean King and Joe Namath popularized the benefits of mid–day meditation for cross–trainers. They lock their doors, unplug their phones, and in a few moments achieve an altered state. Cross–trainers focus on a tennis ball, a mantra, God, their flexibility, strength, endurance, or a perfect physique. Meanwhile their colleagues are spending money on chips and soft–drinks.

> **Rule #1:**
> **Rest More,**
> **Sleep Well**

Rest Revitalizes

Driving on automatic is easier than exploring back roads. For five years I drove six miles on busy thoroughfares until I ventured onto a short–cut back road that halved the distance. I wasted gas and time because I was afraid to risk a new

---

route. In the weight room I trained every other day for ten years without gains. I was the guy begging for a spot and, when someone agreed to help, I broke his back doing negatives. When I turned my third workout day into a rest day, I immediately added strength to my over–trained physique. Muscle fibers are torn down during training and rebuilt during rest.

Resting during the day is important, but a good night's sleep is imperative:

9 Key Points

1. Drink less alcohol and caffeine.

2. Get out of bed if you can't sleep.

3. Follow a schedule.

4. Avoid late evening exercise.

5. Use relaxation techniques.

6. Keep bright light out of your bedroom at night and go outside in the morning.

7. Try milk, turkey, or other low–fat, high–protein foods as a late night snack.

8. Don't look at your alarm clock.

9. Avoid heavy, spicy foods at night.

Be Consistent

Rule #2:
Consistency

I rarely miss a workout. It's the first thing I do each day. I begin at 4:00 a.m. when nobody can see me. There is no waiting in line. It took about two months of yawning to reach my maximum performance, but now I can complete a heavy–duty workout in an hour. I look forward to a.m. gut–busting workouts because the hardest part of my day is over.

Spice It Up

Rule #3:
Variety

To enhance your cross–training performance, vary your workouts. My muscle–strengthening program began when I was thirteen years old. I was a television addict. During commercials I did push–ups. Now, once a month I cross–train a push–up routine to replace bench–press day. Two hundred push–ups using a variety of hand positions trains muscles from different angles.

Mental Preparation

Focus on your training or dissociate from the pain. Monks endure discomfort in a static posture for hours. They still their bodies to focus their minds. Elite cross–training athletes do likewise. In many cross–training activities there are no time–outs, substitutions, or coaching. Long–distance runners, swimmers, cyclists, and skiers spend hours each day alone with their thoughts. Some distract themselves with Metallica, foreign–language tapes, or talk–radio. One world–class ultra–distance cyclist focuses on the white line in front of his tire.

Early research by sport psychologist William Morgan demonstrated that elite athletes "focused in" on their muscles while their also–ran counterparts dissociated. Winning cyclists pay attention to physical measures including miles per hour, revolutions per minute, heart rate, and breathing. "Psychlists" enjoy visualization, dissociation, muscle relaxation, and cognitive restructuring. I use a combination of both. During the first phase of my workout, I dissociate by transporting myself into a pleasant scene. During the last phase, I focus on my form, muscle Z–bands splitting, and engorged muscle fibers. I may cycle the same stretch of road, but each lap is different. My thoughts are never the same.

Rule #4:
Time Flies When
You Change Your
Mind

Instinctive Training

I'm probably one of the few competitive cyclists who doesn't use a training log, heart–rate monitor, or speedometer. I train by instinct. If I feel good, I ride fast. Some call it perceived exertion. Rating of perceived exertion (RPE) is a subjective gauge developed by Borg to prevent overtraining--a yardstick for training and performance. The Borg Scale utilizes a twenty point scale:

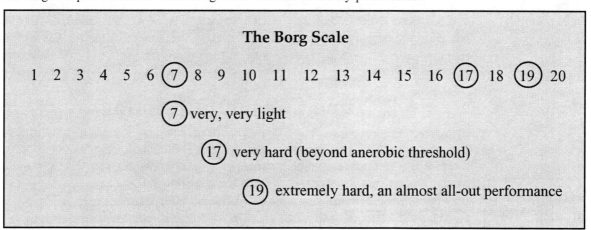

The Borg Scale

1 2 3 4 5 6 ⑦ 8 9 10 11 12 13 14 15 16 ⑰ 18 ⑲ 20

⑦ very, very light

⑰ very hard (beyond anerobic threshold)

⑲ extremely hard, an almost all-out performance

Dissociation to Music

According to the Aerobics and Fitness Association of America, training to music can bring about good health, motivation, and harmony. Several studies have demonstrated the benefits of cross–training to music. A treadmill study at Ohio State University confirmed that exercisers felt less perceived exertion when they ran to music. A study reported in the Journal of Sports Medicine and Physical Fitness showed that exercisers performed better to relaxing music. Relaxing music makes the exercise seem less difficult, allowing the participant to continue longer.

Fine-Tune Your Program

If the weather is nasty for several consecutive days, indoor training can keep you fit. According to Arnie Baker, M.D., a San Diego cycling coach and United States national masters champion, you can get all the workout you need on a home trainer. Training on the road can be somewhat haphazard. Traffic lights, barking dogs, and potholes can slow you down. Training partners may interfere with your program. Baker claims competitive athletes need a track or an indoor trainer to fine–tune their program.

Indoor Fantasy

Indoor workouts are a different world. Running on a treadmill can be mind–altering. But there is no stimulation. You must create it. Indoor training for some requires a fantasy world of books and videos. My favorite rainy–day activity is to rent a two–hour video, fill up my water bottles, turn on the fan, and ride my stationary bike until the movie's over.

Virtual Cycling

Virtual reality (VR) cyclists can spin down winding roads, around lakes, and through small towns. The pedal resistance increases depending on the terrain. If the VR cyclist leans, the seat tilts causing an on–screen turn. If the VR cyclist goes fast he'll actually feel wind in his face.

Cycling in Cyberspace

At the other end of the indoor spectrum, a Race Across America (RAAM) winner stationary–cycled facing a blank wall. Another two–time RAAM winner rode for hours in his basement on rollers, <u>in the dark!</u>

Time Consuming Hobby

Completing the Race Across America gave me a sense of expectation for future ultra–endurance events in terms of saddle sores, bruised feet, and numb hands. Cardiovascular experts advised that a strong aerobic base is an excellent foundation for high mileage training. I followed their recommendations by riding one hundred miles daily in six hours. On weekends I rode six hours straight. On weekdays I split my workout into a three–hour, fifty–mile morning ride followed by an identical evening session. When my wife and I had our fourth baby, Susanna, I had no intention of giving up my dream to finish in the top five of the RAAM; but I became increasingly aware of time commitments.

Rule #5: Quality, Not Quantity

Slow Mega-Miles

Cycling had been my life. I loved to train. I was addicted. I chronically over–trained and didn't know it. I completed my hundred-mile training rides but wasn't getting faster. My work/time ratio had to increase. A cycling magazine inspired me to pedal faster. To increase miles per hour, it was hammer time. I shortened my weight workouts, running, jumping rope, and cycling. But I increased my intensity.

Fast but Good

If you choose a slow pace, you must spend more time per session or train more days per week. Accelerate your cross–training performance by spending <u>less</u> time training. When you work out, less is more. If you work out at a higher intensity, you spend less time exercising. It is truly a paradox; but to get the most bang for your buck and increase the productivity of your cross–training, shorten your routine. But go faster.

Everybody's Doing It

I found support for this shorter–faster style of training in the running, strength training, and body–building literature. Seventy–mile–a–week runners cut their mileage in half, allowing them to run faster and develop fewer running related injuries. Modern body–builders have changed their programs from two–hour, high–volume training to an hour of high–intensity, single–set–to–failure routines. Top level power lifters spend only fifteen minutes actually hoisting iron.

Intensity is Mental

Powering your program is as much mental as physical. Mental preparation is crucial to increase the intensity of your workouts. A high level of arousal is required for high–intensity training. Switching from long–slow distance, high–volume to speedy, high–intensity requires discipline. Recently, professional athletes have been reprimanded for using stimulants to create this heightened state. If you feel sluggish or too relaxed, you cannot power–up. Before heading out the door, visualize explosiveness. Get pumped!

Listen to Your Body

But be sure to warm up for five to ten minutes. Gradually increase your intensity until you reach a steady state. Then go hard and fast, approaching your anaerobic threshold (AT). AT is the level of effort just below where the muscles suffer a large increase in debilitating lactic acid. If you proceed beyond your AT, you will feel lactic acid searing through your muscles. Monitor your breathing and heart rate. Correlate these with your RPE to bring out your best. Your RPE will be slightly uncomfortable as you push closer to your AT. Breathe deeply from your diaphragm. Soon your RPE will be your indicator for increasing your steady state to approach your AT.

Recover

Increased intensity will force you to use Type II, fast–twitch muscle fibers you never knew existed. Recruiting these muscle fibers requires more rest between workouts. Taking a rest day may allow you to train harder the day after. If you love to work out and you train every time you get the chance and you are unsure whether you are over–training, you probably are.

Focus

Lackadaisical, grunt–and–groan, mindless cross–training is history. Instead, I'm totally focused. Rather than plodding through long–slow distance training sessions, I work out hard and fast. Long gone are the days of not eating enough, forcing my body to consume its own muscle. Rarely does my concentration wane. No longer do I wonder, "Why am I doing this?" My intensity has increased. My calories are up. I'm stronger, faster, and carry less body fat.

Speed-Up

It is a myth that your body burns fat only on long–slow distance training days. The more intense your training, the more calories your body burns long after the completion of your workout. Run ten miles in two hours and you burn about the same number of calories running that same ten miles in one hour. The good news is, when you speed up to ten m.p.h., you continue to burn fat at an accelerated rate allowing you to watch the football game you would have missed had you been running a five m.p.h. pace.

Increase Your Good Cholesterol

You lose body fat when you burn more calories than you take in. The more calories burned, the more pounds shed. Researchers at the Human Energy Research Laboratory at the University of Pittsburgh found another benefit to high intensity training. Twelve runners who ran on treadmills for an hour, first at sixty percent of their maximum and then at seventy–five percent, had a higher level of high–density lipoprotein (HDL-good cholesterol) following the higher–intensity workout.

Rule #6:
Smarter,
Not Harder

Free Time

Now I have more time for my job and family, and there is less tension. I feel balanced, more energetic, and my disposition is better. I anticipate training without feeling totally self-centered. My in–laws are less critical, and drivers don't hassle me because I cycle faster up hills.

Success

Recently I tested my "less is best" approach to cycling in a solo, unpaced, record–ride across Arkansas. I covered about two hundred miles in ten hours despite cross–winds and head–winds ranging from ten to twenty m.p.h. I was extremely happy with my performance and I highly recommend speed training.

Plan

Be careful. Lack of planning leads to a wandering style, pulling you back to your comfortable slow pace. Keep a record of workouts. Develop a goal for intensity. Without a plan you may get lazy and train slower. Within a few weeks you inadvertently fall back into your high–volume, less–productive training.

Intensity is Addicting

This being said, there is nothing wrong with a one–day–a–week, mind–altering, ultra–distance, mantra–like, nature stroll. However, following a few months of power– training, it's hard to slow down. It is difficult to let go of newfound intensity. You naturally work harder and smarter. When you slack off, you feel lazy.

(To monitor your indoor training progress see Chart J on page 125.)

(To monitor your cycling progress see Chart K on page 127.)

Attitude

Positive Attitude

Cross–training smart is more than physical. Attitude affects cross–training workouts and immune systems as well according to Dr. Larry Dossey. Smile, think positive thoughts, believe you can improve; and your chances increase significantly. Ancient medicine men tuned into their patients' belief–systems before formulating a cure. Dwight Stones wouldn't jump until he saw a mental picture of himself clearing the bar. Medical doctors prescribe placebos. Millionaires attribute success to attitude. Elite athletes and entertainers testify to the power of attitude. The University of Chicago's Csikszentmihalyi believes that cultivating a positive attitude in the face of adversity fosters "un–self–conscious self–assurance".

Programs

Successful motivators talk about basic truths. They share a common sense, sometimes Biblical, approach to achieving peak performance. Their programs include relaxation techniques, concentration training, visualization, behavior modification, self–talk strategies, and self–esteem enhancement.

Expense

Group meditation and spiritual programs have made millions of dollars for their founders. Leaders attract followers into their programs by promising a speedy path to self–discovery. If you pay enough, you can learn to walk on hot coals or break a brick. Most drop out, but not before their pockets are emptied.

Short Term Results

Spin–offs are everywhere, but there seems no sure, one–size–fits–all method of building and keeping a positive attitude. People can lose weight, but less than five percent keep it off; similarly, during a motivational seminar, participants are fired up, but try checking back on them in a few days.

Periodization

Krause said our attitudes affect ourperceptions, which affect our feelings, which affect our performances. But attitude like motivation is ever changing. So is performance. You cannot be at your best all the time. Plan peak performances to coincide with optimum attitude and motivation. Chart your progress leading to your cross–training goal.

Circadian Rhythms

Cross–trainers watch their body clocks for performance advantages. Circadian rhythms affect hormones, urinary excretion, blood pressure, heart rate, vigor, alertness, body temperature, metabolism, and sleep. These rhythms follow a twenty– four hour, light–dark cycle. Body temperature, arousal, strength, and flexibility peak late in the day. Sport performance improves over the course of the day, suggesting the lack of world records before noon. Research shows a ten percent increase in strength and aerobic power for men and women tested later in the day.

Trust

Trust your body to do the right thing. Maslow's Self Actualization Theory is the foundation of the United States Army slogan, "Be all you can be." A weekend hacker or a pro player sets a cross–training goal and decides whether the pain required to get there is worth it. Once you get close to your goal, believe that you deserve it. You do! Optimism increases your chances for achievement by bolstering persistence according to Martin Seligman, a psychologist at the University of Pennsylvania.

Steps to Reformation

Psychologist James Prochaska defines four stages we must go through to improve our attitude to increase performance.

1. **Precontemplation** – Concerned but afraid to do anything.

2. **Contemplation** – Ambivalent, but acquiring more information.

3. **Preparation** – Taking the first step toward a change.

4. **Action** – Diving headlong into your new program.

Another Program

A similar program, PACE (Physician–Based Assessment and Counseling for Exercise) is more specific to cross–training. PACE describes a Precontemplator as one who does not cross–train and does not intend to start. A Contemplator does not cross–train but is thinking about starting. An Active individual cross–trains moderately or vigorously several times a week. The PACE program identifies several roadblocks and how to overcome them:

```
                              PACE

    Roadblock              Overcome it.

    1.  No time        Trade thirty minutes of TV for cross–training three
                       times per week.

    2.  No fun         Start a hobby that keeps you moving.

    3.  Too tired      Cross–training energizes.  Try it!

    4.  Boring         Use headphones and look at the scenery.

    5.  Get sore       Start gradually and stretch after each cross-training
                       workout.
```

Find a Passion

What is your cross–training passion? If you don't have one, search for it as if for the first time. View every activity with a fresh perspective. Jim Gavin, Ph.D., says the easiest way to enjoy a cross–training program is to find one that complements you. Tennis players are sociable and spontaneous while weight trainers tend to be disciplined and aggressive. Runners may lack sociability and spontaneity, but they are extremely disciplined. Golfers are sociable and competitive but may have little discipline. Yoga students are mentally focused but not very aggressive. What are your characteristics and talents? Are you sociable or focused? Do you possess exceptional flexibility or strength?

> **Rule #7:**
> **Find An Activity**
> **That Complements**
> **You.**

Muscular Endurance

Test yourself. How many push–ups can you do? How many crunches? If you can do five pushups and five crunches, add one each week until you can do twenty pushups and twenty crunches. Maintain perfect form and move through a full range of motion. Time your breathing so you exhale on the exertion. Perform both push–ups and crunches without resting between repetitions.

Stamina

Can you walk for thirty minutes? Walk ten minutes a day for a week. Each week add one minute until you are walking thirty minutes.

Flexibility

Are you flexible? Stretch each day and measure your progress each month. In a year you may be surprised at your increased flexibility. Stretch gradually. Stretch after you warm–up and after you complete your workout. Stretch to the point of tension, never pain.

Reasons to Cross-Train

1. You'll meet new friends.

2. You can cross-train with your family anytime, anywhere.

3. Cross-training improves your fitness and self-esteem.

4. Cross-training is a flexible method of fitness.

5. Cross-training helps you lose body-fat and tone muscles.

6. Cross-training dissolves stress.

7. Cross training is inexpensive and easy.

(To monitor your addiction–replacement strategy see Chart L on page 129.)

Indoor Training

Mode of Exercise	Date	Time	Intensity	Duration	Feelings

Chart

Cycling

Date	Time	Duration	Intensity	Mileage	Feelings

CROSS-TRAINING

Chart

ADDICTION-REPLACEMENT

Old Habit or Attitude	When	Where	Cross–Training Replacement

CROSS-TRAINING REVIEW

11

Physical Training

Picture Bruce Lee without flexibility. A scrawny, stick–figure, fighting machine. Or imagine Evander Holyfield as a cruiserweight what's–his–name before beefing up into an incredible heavyweight. Fat is okay if you enjoy sumo, and skinny is in if you're an emaciated, Auschwitz–like marathon runner. But the times they–are–a–changing. Contemporary, intelligent athletes know they won't sacrifice sports performance by enhancing speed, endurance, flexibility, or by obtaining slabs of good–looking muscle. NBA basketball players and major leaguers resemble bodybuilders. Elite runners are stretching to lengthen their stride. Golfers travel in vans equipped with the latest in fitness paraphernalia. And tennis players work out on Nautilus machines.

Elite racket sport players cross–train for improved performance. Consider a tennis player's disproportionately huge arm. Cross–training flexibility and strength promote symmetry and protect joints. Improved fitness hasn't hurt Andre Agassi's win–loss record. He credits his personal trainer with strengthening his booming serve. Martina Navatrilova's cross–training program has been mimicked by aspiring athletes all over the world.

Olympic gold medalist speed skater Dan Jansen cross–trained to build huge, powerful legs. Bird–legged bodybuilders throughout the world may try speed skating as their magic cross–training bullet. Mesomorphs such as Hershel Walker say they developed tremendous physiques from cross–training pushups andcrunches during television commercials. Oriental karate masters claimed they grew powerful muscles by cross–training dynamic tension exercises with their martial arts techniques. Jamaicans' muscular bodies are a product of good genetics, clean eating, and cross–training walking with farming.

Tough–Guys

Walk into a gym and look around. It's easy to spot the athletes who cross–train properly and those who don't. Tough–guys power the weights. They grunt, and spit, and punch through six, fast repetitions. Spotters yell at them, and they talk tough for several minutes between sets.

Racket Sports

Racket sport players own a single, vascular, muscled–up appendage. They do twelve repetitions in a single circuit, zipping through the machines in no time. Racket sport players are generally lean except for a bulging midriff. They are intimidated by the powerfully built tough–guys.

Endurance Athletes

Endurance athletes are serious about their workouts. They can run for miles but have difficulty touching their toes. They run on the treadmills, stair climbers, and stationary bicycles glancing at their watches to check heart rates. After toweling their soaked cardio–machines, they hustle through the weights, lifting light, with lots of repetitions, fearful of gaining muscle. They avoid tough–guys but are not bothered by racket sports people.

Do It Right

From time to time a traditional sports person will miraculously be transformed into a tried and true cross–trainer. An endurance athlete buckles down to some heavy stretching, a tough–guy tries a stair climber, or a racket sportsplayer performs three straight sets on the bench. If these magic moments continue, the endurance athlete lengthens her stride, the tough–guy develops cardiovascular endurance, and the racket sport player gains strength.

No Expectations

I was invited to spread the good news about cross–training to high school single–sport athletes. I arrived early, hoping to observe high school in the 1990's. A light touch on my shoulder accompanied a stern warning: "Visitors must check in at the office." When I explained to the woman that I was the cross–training speaker, she hurried me into the principal's office. The principal greeted me with, "These kids won't listen to you. They don't listen to anyone." A teacher remarked, "Didn't I almost run you over?" She reminded me how my bike slid sideways off a curb and landed inches in front of the front wheel of her Suburban. Fortunately she heard me screaming and banging on her bumper. We had a good laugh, but she didn't expect the kids to take me seriously.

Abdominal Strength

Following my introduction, horseplay began. I pointed to an offender. "Come up here. I need a volunteer," I yelled. The student was bigger than I thought. He slowly arose to catcalls and whistles from peers. I asked him to punch me in the stomach. He hit me pretty hard. I said, "Is that your best shot? Try again." The audience fell silent. This time he nailed me but was incredulous that I was still standing. "Now it's my turn" I said, and reared back to punch as his classmates roared with laughter. He helped me demonstrate a tummy resistance exercise guaranteed to produce a flat, muscular stomach in thirty days:

Crunches:

Lie on your back with your knees bent, feet flat on the floor, your chin resting on your chest, and arms crossed on your chest. Curl your head and shoulders off the floor upward and forward until the point before the small of your back starts to leave the floor. Hold for three seconds, then concentrate on your abdominals on the way down. The range of motion is only a few inches so you don't have to raise your torso as you would a regular sit–up. Do ten repetitions.

Reverse Crunches:

Lie on your back with your knees bent, feet flat on the floor, and hands under your hips. Keep your knees together as you bring them toward your chest. Hold for three seconds, then let your feet slowly fall back towards the floor as you concentrate on your lower abdominals. Do ten repetitions.

Calisthenics

To motivate the athletes to do calisthenics, I explained that my first cross-training experience took place when I was their age. At 7 a.m. my high school coach pushed us through a high-intensity, muscular endurance program. Our goal was to max out on five events which included one-hundred situps in two minutes, sixty consecutive push-ups, thirty pull-ups, a ten foot standing broad-jump, and a sixty-meter shuttle run, all performed in less than thirty minutes, three days a week. One set to failure catapulted us into the best shapes of our lives. Without touching a weight, our physiques resembled the natural bodybuilding competitors of today.

Strength Programs Work

Westcott's 1993 research demonstrated that ten fourteen-year-old girls and boys added three to four pounds of muscle and lost two pounds of fat on an eight-week strength training program. They did one to three sets of exercises for each body part two to three days a week. The bad news is that the 1994 Presidents Council On Physical Fitness and Sport reported half of the girls and one-third of the boys aged six to sixteen cannot do a single pull-up. Only fifty percent of youngsters exercise regularly.

Strength Improves Sport

I described to the athletes how my tennis coach at Penn State didn't want me to cross–train with weights, but I didn't listen. I was the most muscular but not the best player on the team. The coach could never find me because I was in a weight room or running. Maybe I was ahead of my time because today all the top players cross–train. Steffi Graf and Pete Sampras spend almost as much time cross–training as on the tennis court.

Imagery

I pointed to another athlete and explained how important concentration is. I said, "Imagine my hands are a magnet and your back is made of steel. Feel the magnet pulling stronger and stronger. Pulling you back off your feet. Concentrate on the magnet, nothing to bother you or disturb you, just listen to my voice." To his amazement he flew back into my hands. The athletes chose partners and were surprised at their ability to focus on the magnet.

Roll With the Punches

I greeted my next athlete with a loudkiai (karate yell). He jumped back and the others laughed. I told him to put his right hand on his chest and his left hand on his tummy. Then we both inhaled and exhaled, slowly and deliberately, so that only our left hands moved. We inhaled and exhaled through our noses pausing for two seconds (without holding our breath) allowing our exhalation to come to a natural and unforced conclusion. We allowed all of the air to escape from our lungs before starting another inhalation. We breathed from our diaphragms so that we could selectively relax all of our muscles. Without warning, I kicked him lightly on his arm. Caught off–guard, he tightened and stumbled. After I helped him up, I showed him how to relax and roll with a punch. In a few minutes he was able to defend himself against a flurry of punches and kicks.

Muscle and Flexibility

My next volunteer athlete helped me demonstrate partner resistance exercises. She pushed and I pulled to tone her muscles. I handed her some dumbells, and she repeated the exercises on her own. Next I stretched her arms and legs like Gumby. She learned that if she stretched two minutes a day, in six months she could perform incredible feats of flexibility.

No Shortcuts

Several athletes perked up when I said I knew the secrets to a sleek body. Years ago at the University of Massachusetts, researchers studied men who performed up to three hundred sit–ups a day for a month and found that they lost almost no fat. I suggested to eat low–fat, exercise, and refrain from alcohol. We discussed eating fruits, vegetables, cereals, grains, breads, lean meats, and non–fat dairy products. Most knew to stay away from fat and sugar. But many didn't know that adding a few minutes of walking, and weight training, to their existing sports program could be extremely beneficial.

Coping with Adversity

With just a few minutes remaining, I spoke about the importance of following our dreams. I talked about the Race Across America with reference to persistence in the face of adversity, and noted that quitting once makes it easier to quit again, and that success breeds success. I suggested each of them dive into their sport and set a cross–training goal. Athletes summed up by practicing toning exercises, aerobics, concentration training, and relaxation.

Pay Attention

Driving home I was euphoric, hoping to have reached a few of these athletes. My pedal to the metal, my mind on everything but the road, I imagined how the athletes might apply cross–training principles to their lives. A police siren brought me back to reality. My seminar fee helped pay my speeding ticket.

(To monitor your sports training progress see Chart M on page 139.)

Cross-Training Survival Tips

1. Visualize a peak performance but cross–train a variety of alternatives.

2. Stay balanced. Cross–train your physical, mental, spiritual, social, and emotional life.

3. Push hard, but relaxation is an integral part of your cross–training effort.

4. Stay focused, but cultivate a broad cross–training base.

5. Trim away non–essential activities so you can concentrate on your cross–training priorities.

6. Cross–train your work with play.

7. Take a deep breath and relax between cross–training efforts.

8. Talk to yourself nicely during cross–training activity.

Continued

---

9. Be confident in your cross-training lifestyle.

10. If things are not "taking off", revitalize yourself for your next cross-training adventure.

11. Cross-training is not just physical and mental activity, it is a new and exciting approach to living.

12. Spend at least five minutes daydreaming each day. Turn off the radio on your way to work.

13. Eat frequently through the day. Try to consume three good meals and three mini-meals. At each sitting eat one serving of protein (egg whites, chicken, fish, turkey, lean red meat), one starchy carbohydrate (potato, brown rice, beans, peas, corn, etc.), and one cruciferous vegetable (broccoli, leafy greens, etc.).

14. Work out with weights twice a week. Do aerobics three times a week. Stretch every other day.

15. Breathe from your diaphragm whenever you catch yourself panting anxiously.

16. Memorize a favorite quote from the Bible or a Chinese saying to calm yourself.

17. Feel honestly exhausted from a day well spent.

18. Move. Life is too short to spend half of it sitting around overeating.

19. If you don't feel like cross-training, just tie your shoes and get started. Once you break a sweat, you'll be glad you did.

20. Let your children watch you cross-train. You're their best rolemodel.

21. Cross-train at different times of the day to discover when you enjoy it the most.

22. If you cross-train alone, work out with a buddy; or if you usually train with others, go it alone.

23. Intersperse high and low-impact movements. Your body will thank you.

(To monitor your calisthenics progress see Chart N on page 141.)

Chart

SPORT TRAINING

Sport	Date	Time	Duration	Intensity	Who With?	Feelings

CALISTHENICS

Exercise	Date	Time	Perceived Exertion	Feelings

CROSS-TRAINING

CROSS-TRAINING DO'S and DON'TS

Do it now

Don't sit down

Don't open the refrigerator for excitement

Don't go into the kitchen between meals on a rainy day

Don't order desserts when you eat out

Don't eat junk food at home

Don't drink water only when you're thirsty

Do drink water when you are hungry

Don't work out with your spouse's best friend

Don't lift weights for the same muscle group more than twice a week

Do participate in two different cardiovascular activities in a day

Don't eat sweets at snack time if you're a sugar–holic

Don't use a gigantic bowl and spoon to eat

Do eat more to exercise

Don't go to a spectator sport hungry

Do eat before you go out

CROSS-TRAINING

CROSS-TRAINING FOR SPORT

To improve your sport performance on a 30 minute time–limited, twice a week schedule:

Date	Plyometrics	Compound-Consecutive-Circuit	Stretching	(10 min.)	(15 min.)	(5 min.)

CROSS-TRAINING

QUESTIONS

How can cross–training improve your life?

How can cross–training increase your energy?

How can cross–training improve your health?

How can cross–training affect the shape of your body?

Do you dissociate or focus–in on your cross–training efforts?   Explain.

Can you change your negative thoughts into a cross–training adventure?   Explain.

Name two cross–training programs that contribute to your fitness.   Explain.

Name your favorite five foods to fuel your cross–training performance.

Is there an emotional, social, and spiritual component to your cross–training efforts?   Explain.

Do you have a cross–training role model?

continued

How can you fit cross–training into your busy schedule?

What is your cross–training background?

How can you change your play into cross–training?

Describe the strength component to your cross–training program.

Describe the flexibility component to your cross–training program.

Describe the endurance component to your cross–training program.

Describe the stress–management component to your cross–training program.

Describe the nutrition component to your cross–training program.

How can you get friends and family involved in cross–training?

How do you psych–up for your cross training event?

Can flexibility training enhance your cross–training?

Which is better. Cross–training harder or cross–training smarter? Explain.

CHECKLIST

Check yes or no to the following questions.

Goal Setting: Do you set short and long term goals? Yes_____ No _____

Aerobics: Do you do at least twenty minutes of an aerobic activity three to four times each week? Yes_____ No _____

Resistance Training: Do you lift weights or do calisthenics working each body part twice a week? Yes _____ No _____

Stretching: Do you stretch all of your muscles at least three times a week? Yes_____ No _____

Eating: Do you eat several complete meals throughout the day, cutting down on fat and sugar? Yes _____ No _____

Sleeping: Do you get six to eight hours of sleep each night? Yes _____ No _____

Stress Management: Do you use a coping strategy when stress levels are high? Yes_____ No _____

Change: When you get in a rut, do you change your program? Yes _____ No _____

Social: Are you getting enough of, and the right kind of, social activity? Yes_____ No _____

Spiritual: Is your spiritual life meeting your needs? Yes _____ No _____

Emotional: Are you experiencing a wide range of emotions? Yes _____ No _____

Boredom: Can you keep yourself occupied? Yes _____ No_____

Cognitive Dissonance: Can you handle an evil temptation? Yes _____ No _____

Fulfillment: Are you happy? Yes _____ No _____

CROSS-TRAINING

ISSUES in the YEAR 2000

The following topics are currently being researched by the National Institute of Health's Alternative Medicine Division:

1. Relaxation combined with visualization may induce brain wave changes in patients with chronic low–back pain.

2. Relaxation coupled with guided imagery may bolster the immune system.

3. Guided imagery may enhance the immune function of women treated for breast cancer.

4. Imagery may help asthma patients by improving airflow, reducing symptoms and the need for medications.

5. "Therapeutic touch" may help maintain immune function in highly stressed people.

6. Eight weeks of daily tai chi exercise may improve balance in people with mild balance disorders.

7. Meditation, a special diet, and exercise may prevent illness and improve general health.

8. Weekly practice of yoga may help heroin addicts remain in methadone treatments, reduce their criminal activity, and decrease their use of alcohol and illicit drugs.

9. Breathing techniques may help adolescents and adults who have obsessive–compulsive disorder.

10. Biofeedback techniques may offer relief to patients with low–back, facial, or jaw pain.

11. Biofeedback may help control stress–induced hyperglycemia and reduce the need for insulin in people with insulin–dependentdiabetes.

12. When people pray on behalf of a specific individual, those prayers may enhance that person's recovery.

CROSS-TRAINING

CONTRACT

I _____ WILL CHOOSE AT LEAST TWO ACTIVITIES PRESENTED IN CROSS-TRAINING AS PARTIAL FULFILLMENT OF THE REQUIREMENTS FOR MY CROSS-TRAINING PROGRAM ON THIS _____ DAY OF _____ IN THE YEAR _____.

SIGNED _____

OBJECTIVE TEST QUESTIONS

Answer True or False to the left of each question. Answers may be found within the Cross–Training Text.

1. Fats are the most efficient fuel source for your cross–training muscles. T _____ F _____

2. Warm–up after you stretch. T _____ F _____

3. Work out the same muscle groups daily in your cross–weight training program. T _____ F _____

4. Cross–training with walking burns fat. T _____ F _____

5. Walking behind a push mower is aerobic cross–training. T _____ F _____

6. Lifting weights is the best cross–training aerobic exercise. T _____ F _____

7. We are biologically designed to be cross–trainers. T _____ F _____

8. Belly laughter does not relieve stress. T _____ F _____

9. To lose body fat and retain muscle, eat one meal a day. T _____ F _____

10. Cross–weight training can make you more flexible. T _____ F _____

11. Cardiovascular disease is preventable. T _____ F _____

12. Cross–training at your target heart rate is the only way to burn calories. T _____ F _____

13. Sit–ups is the best way to cross–train fat from your waistline. T _____ F _____

14. Cross–weight training slows your metabolism. T _____ F _____

15. Cross–training with plyometrics can cause injury. T _____ F _____

continued

16. Your first line for injury prevention on a walking program is purchasing a shoe fitted to your walking style. T _____ F _____

17. Prayer, mental preparation, or visualization has no effect on your cross–training performance. T _____ F _____

18. It is impossible to have well–defined muscles and cross–train aerobically. T _____ F _____

19. Cross–training with weights decreases your flexibility and aerobic endurance. T _____ F _____

20. Cross–training strength, flexibility, and endurance is too time consuming for the average American. T _____ F _____

21. Cross–training physical activities does not benefit your brain. T _____ F _____

22. Cross–training with members of your family is not a good idea. T _____ F _____

23. It is impossible to lose two pounds of fat each week on a cross–training eating and exercise program. T _____ F _____

24. Gender differences make cross–training totally different for men and women. T _____ F _____

25. Cross–training is a habit like brushing your teeth. T _____ F _____

26. A cross–trainer who associates will be a better athlete than one who dissociates. T _____ F _____

27. Your ability to handle stress has no bearing on your cross–training program. T _____ F _____

28. Your eating plan has no effect on your cross–training performance. T _____ F _____

29. Humor is detrimental to your cross–training efforts. T _____ F _____

30. All cross–training athletes train at least 6 hours daily. T _____ F _____

31. Balance is not a part of your cross–training program. T _____ F _____

32. Cross–training demands a lonely lifestyle. T _____ F _____

33. Cross–training in solitude is more beneficial than team cross–training. T _____ F _____

34. There are no absolutes when it comes to cross–training. T _____ F _____

35. It is better for kids to specialize in a single sport rather than cross–train. T _____ F _____

36. Cross–training makes you well–rounded which is unhealthy. T _____ F _____

continued

37. Cross–training is too physically demanding for the young and the elderly. T _____ F _____

38. Muscle maintenance does not enhance a cross–training program. T _____ F _____

39. There is no one way to cross–train. T _____ F _____

40. Cross–training is a lifestyle. T _____ F _____

41. Your target weight should depend on what you weigh on the scale. T _____ F _____

42. Lose weight fast. T _____ F _____

43. Shop for foods when you are hungry. T _____ F _____

44. Plan your meals in advance. T _____ F _____

45. It is a good idea to go for a walk after a meal. T _____ F _____

46. Dieting is the only way to lose fat. T _____ F _____

47. Muscle weighs more than fat. T _____ F _____

48. Missing breakfast is a good weight loss strategy. T _____ F _____

49. Weight training makes you slow and muscle bound. T _____ F _____

50. Swimming is the best choice of exercise for losing fat. T _____ F _____

Chapter Reference

1. SPORT PERFORMANCE

a. **Power**: Chapter 4: Plyometrics will make you quicker, stronger, and improve your vertical jump.

b. **Flexibility**: Chapter 6: Stretching will increase your agility, resilience, and decrease your chance of injury.

c. **Endurance**: Chapter 8: Aerobic activities will increase your stamina and decrease your body fat.

d. **Eating**: Chapter 2: A good eating plan will increase your energy, strength, and decrease your body fat.

e. **Strength**: Chapter 3: Resistance training will make you stronger and more powerful.

f. **Mental Training**: Chapter 5: Mental preparation will increase your ability to relax, concentrate, and deal with pain.

2. GETTING FIT

a. **Flexibility**: Chapter 6: Five minutes of easy stretching will improve your posture and enhance your overall sense of well being.

b. **Strength**: Chapter 3: Thirty minutes of resistance training will increase your metabolism and tone your muscles.

c. **Endurance**: Chapter 8: Twenty minutes of your favorite aerobics will strengthen your heart and lungs and decrease your body fat.

f. **Mental Training**: Chapter 5: Five minute mini–strategies can let you relax and concentrate.

g. **Eating**: Chapter 2: Increase energy and decrease body fat.

CROSS-TRAINING

References

Addiction. (1987) *Aerobics News*. Dallas Institute of Aerobics Research.

American Academy of Pediatrics. (1983) Weight Training and Weight Lifting: Information for the Pediatrician. *Physician and Sports Medicine*. 11.

American Heart Association. (1994) *Heart and Stroke Facts*. Dallas, Texas.

Armstrong, R. (1984) Mechanisms of Exercise–Induced Delayed Onset Muscular Soreness: A Brief Review. *Medicine and Science in Sports Exercise*. Vol. 6.

Barbato, J. (1989) *Mind Body Health Digest*.

Benson, A. (1994) Familiarity Breeds Content. *Runner's World*. Vol. 29. Number 7. November.

Beaulieu, J. (1981) Developing a Stretching Program. *Physician and Sports Medicine*. Vol 9. November.

Benson, H. (1984) *Beyond The Relaxation Response*. Times Books, New York, New York.

Benson, H. (1987) *Your Maximum Mind*. Times Books, New York, New York.

Benson, H. (1993) *The Wellness Book..* Simon & Schuster, New York, New York.

Blair, S. (1989) Physical Fitness and All Cause Mortality. *Journal of the American Medical Association*. Vol. 262.

Blair, S. (1985) Relationships Between Exercise, Physical Activity and Other Health Behaviors. *Public Health Reports*. Vol. 100.

Borg, G. (1973) Perceived Exertion: A Note on History and Methods. *Medicine and Science in Sports and Exercise*. Vol. 5.

Bouchard, C. (1990) Basic and Clinical Aspects of Regional Fat Distribution. *American Journal of Clinical Nutrition*. Vol. 52.

Borysenko, J. (1988) *Minding The Body, Mending The Mind*. Bantam Books, NewYork, New York.

Bray, G. (1992) Pathophysiology of Obesity. *American Journal of Clinical Nutrition*. Vol. 55.

Brody, J. (1988) *Jane Brody's Nutrition Book*. BantamBooks, New York, New York.

Campbell, W. (1994) Increased Energy Requirements and Changes in Body Composition With Resistance Training in Older Adults. *American Journal of Clinical Nutrition*. August.

Carlton, B. (1995) A Radical Idea. *Bicycling*. January. Vol. 36. No. 1.

Clarke, H. (1977) Jogging. *Physical Fitness Research Digest.* January.

Clarke, H. (1977) Swimming and Bicycling. *Physical Fitness Research Digest.* July.

Coleman, E. (1992) *Eating For Endurance.* Bull Publishing, Palo Alto, CA.

Colgan, M. (1993) *Optimum Sports Nutrition.* Advanced Research Press, New York, New York.

Consumer Reports Health Letter. (1990) How to Lose Weight and Keep it Off. *Consumers Union* 2. Vol. 2. February.

Cooper, K. (1994) Natural Health. *Prevention.* Vol. 46, # 9. September issue.

Csikszentmihalyi, M. (1994) *Flow: The Psychology of Optimal Experience..* Simon & Schuster, New York, New York.

Dossey, Larry. (1993) *Healing Words.* Harper Collins, New York, New York.

Edman, K. (1979) *The Effect of Stretch on Contracting Skeletal Muscle Cells.* Cross–Bridge Mechanism in Muscular Contraction. University Park Press, Baltimore, Maryland.

Eichner, E. (1988) Circadian Timekeepers in Sports. *The Physician and Sportsmedicine.* Vol. 16. Number 2.

Evans, W. (1992) Exercise, Nutrition, and Aging. *Journal of Nutrition.* Vol. 122.

Fellingham, G. (1978) Caloric Cost of Walking and Running. *Medicine and Science i n Sports.* Number 2.

Fiatarone, M. (1994) Exercise Training and Nutritional Supplementation for Physical Frailty in Very Elderly People. *New England Journal of Medicine.* Vol. 330. Number 25.

Fleck, S. (1992) Cardiovascular Response to Strength Training. *Strength and Power in Sport.* Oxford Blackwell.

Freidman, M. (1989) A Master Of Moving Meditation. *New Realities.* June issue, pgs. 11–20.

Friden, J. (1981) A Morphological Study of Delayed Muscle Soreness. *Experiencia.* Vol. 37.

Getchel, B. (1992) *A Way of Life..* Macmillan, New York, New York.

Getchel, B. (1980) The Caloric Costs of Rope Skipping and Running. *Physician and Sportsmedicine.* Vol. 8.

Getchel, L. (1968) Energy Cost of Playing Golf. *Archives of Physical Medicine and Rehabilitation.* Vol. 49. Number 1.

Goleman, D. (1988) *The Meditative Mind.* Tarcher. Los Angeles, California.

Goleman, D. (1993) *Mind Body Medicine.* Yonkers, Consumer Reports Books, Yonkers, New York.

Hakkinen, K. (1989) Neuromuscular and Hormonal Adaptations During Strength and Power training. *Journal of Sports Medicine and Physical Fitness.* Vol. 29.

Holt, L. (1970) Comparative Study of Three Stretching Techniques. *Perceptual and Motor Skills.,* Vol. 31.

Hortobgyi, T. (1993) The Effects of Detraining on Power Athletes. *Medicine in Science in Sports and Exercise.* Number 25.

Ice, R. (1992) Amino Acids And Human Performance. *Ultra Cycling.* Vol. l, Number 4. Fall.

Jenkins, D. (1989) Nibbling Versus Gorging: Metabolic Advantages of Increased Meal Frequency. *New England Journal of Medicine.* Vol. 321. Number 14.

Jenkins, R. (1993) Oxidant Stress Aging and Exercise. *Medicine in Science in Sports and Exercise.,* Vol. 25.

Jones, P. (1993) Meal Frequency Effects on Plasma Hormone Concentrations and Cholesterol Synthesis in Humans. *American Journal of Clinical Nutrition.* Vol. 57. Number 6.

Langer, E. (1989) *Mindfulness.* Addison Wesley Pub. Co., New York, New York.

Leonard, G. (1987) Mastery. *Esquire.*

Lichtman, S. (1992) Discrepancy Between Self–Reported and Actual Caloric Intake and Exercise in Obese Subjects. *The New England Journal of Medicine.* Vol. 327. Number 27.

Lieber, R. (1992) *Skeletal Muscle Structure and Function.* Williams and Wilkins, Baltimore, Maryland.

Liebman, B. (1990) Getting Your Vitamins. *Nutrition ActionHealth Letter.* June issue. pgs. 5–7.

Lynch, J. (1994) The Psychology of Running. *Runner's World.* 33 E. Minor St. Emmaus, Pennsylvania. July issue.

Lyons, J. (1978) Cross–Country Skiing. *Journal of the American Medical Association.* Vol. 239 Number 4. January.

Matheny, F. (1994) Floor It. *Bicycling.* December.

McArdle W, Katch, F, and Katch, V. (1991) *Exercise Physiology – Energy, Nutrition, and Human Performance.* Lea & Febiger, Malvern, Pennsylvania.

Mycoskie, P, (1992) *Butter Busters.* Butter Busters Publishing. Arlington, Texas.

Netzer, C.T. (1991) *The Complete Book of Food Counts.* Dell Publishing. New York, New York.

Ornish, D. (1990) *Can Lifestyle Changes Reverse Coronary Heart Disease?"* Lancet. Vol. 336.

Ornstein, R., & Sobel, D. (1987) *The Healing Brain.* Touchstone, New York, New York.

O'Shea, J. (1982) Bicycle Interval Training for Cardiovascular Fitness. *Physician and Sportsmedicine.* Vol. 10.

Osgarden, J. (1994) Have It Your Way. *Bicycling.* December.

Prevention Magazine. (1994) The Prevention Index 1994: A Report Card on the Nation's Health.

Schultz, P. (1979) *Flexibility: Day of the Static Stretch.* November.

Seabourne, T.G. (1986) Cross Court Training. *TaeKwonDo Times.* November issue. pg. 68, 69.

Seabourne, T.G. (1987) Deck Of Fitness. *Better Health and Living.* February issue. pg. 16.

Seabourne, T.G. (1986) Mental Kicks. *Superfit.* Fall issue. pg. 6.

Seabourne, T.G. (1986) Psychological Training for Women. *Fighting Woman News.* September issue. New York, New York.

Seabourne, T.G. (1987) Seeing Is Believing. *Slimmer.* April issue. pgs. 34–36.

Seabourne, T.G. (1987) Take The Time For A Proper Diet. *Triathlon Magazine.* September issue. pgs.14,15.

Seabourne, T.G. (1981) The Effects of Relaxation and Imagery Training on Karate Performance. *Karate Illustrated.* March issue.

Seabourne, T.G. (1994) One More Rep! *Exercise For Men Only.* September issue. Chelo Pub. Inc. 350 Fifth Ave, Suite 8216, New York, New York

Seabourne, T.G. (1987) Understanding the Body–Mind Relationship. *Houston Health and Fitness News.* October issue. pg. 38

Seabourne, T.G. (1987) Visualizing Yourself As A Success. *Houston Health and Fitness News.* December issue. pg. 17

Seabourne, T.G., and Herndon, E. (1986) *Self Defense: A Body–Mind Approach..* Gorsuch–Scarisbrick. Scottsdale, Arizona.

Seabourne, T.G. and Mclaughlin, C.V. (1989) Managing Stress While Performing Police Tasks. *Your Virginia State Trooper Magazine.* pg. 78,79.

Seabourne, T.G., and Jackson, A. (1981) Effects of Visuo–motor Behavior Rehearsal, Relaxation, and Imagery on Karate Performance. *Journal of Sport Psychology*. Vol. 3. Number 3.

Seabourne, T.G., Weinberg, R.S., (1985) Martial Mind Games: Can You Psyche Yourself Into Winning? *Inside Karate*. March issue.

Seabourne, T.G., Weinberg, R.S., and Jackson, A., (1985) Effect of Arousal and Relaxation Instructions Prior to the Use of Imagery. *Journal of Sport Behavior*.

Seabourne, T.G., Weinberg, R. (1983) Mental Practice: Research Shows It May Improve Your Physical Performance. *Kick Illustrated*. September issue.

Seabourne, T.G., Weinberg, R.S., and Jackson, A. (1983) Effect of Individualized Practice and Training of Visuo–motor Behavior Rehearsal In Enhancing Karate Performance. *Journal of Sport Behavior*. Vol. 7. Number 2. pgs. 58–67.

Seabourne, T.G., Weinberg, R.S., and Jackson, A. (1985) The Effects of Guided VMBR vs. Individualized VMBR Training on Karate Performance. *Karate Illustrated*.

Seabourne, T.G., Weinberg, R.S., Jackson, A., Suinn, R., (1985) Effect of Individualized, Nonindividualized, and Packaged Intervention Strategies on Athletic Performance. *Journal of Sport Psychology*. Vol. 7. Numer 1.

Sheats, C. (1992) *Lean Bodies*. The Summit Group. Fort Worth, Texas

Shepherd, B. (1988) Dealing With Our Addictions. *Yoga Journal*. December issue. pg. 103

Sherman, C. (1994) Stress: How to Help Patients Cope. *The Physician and Sports Medicine*. Vol 22. Number 7. July.

Shermer, M. (1994) An Inspiration. *Ultra Cycling*. Summer issue. 2761 North Marengo Ave. Altadena, California.

Siegel, B. (1986) *Love, Medicine, And Miracles*. Harper & Row. NewYork, New York.

Simonton, C. (1992) *Getting Well Again*. Bantam Books, NewYork, New York.

Stensland, S. (1990) Simplifying the Calculation of Body Mass Index for Quick Reference. *Journal of the American Dietetic Association*. Vol. 90.

Sullivan, D. (1994) Thrills Without Spills. *Health*. Vol. 8. Number 6. October issue.

Town, G. (1980) The Effect of Rope Skipping Rate on Energy Expenditure of Males and Females. *Medicine and Science in Sports and Exercise*.

University of Victoria. Cycling Fat. *Canadian Journal of Sports Science*; Vol. 13. Number 4.

Weinberg, R.S., Seabourne, T.G., and Jackson, A. (1982) Effects of Visuo–Motor Behavior Rehearsal on State–Trait Anxiety and Performance: Is Practice Important? *Journal of Sport Behavior* Vol. 5. Number 4. pgs. 209–218.

Wescott, W. (1994) Why Every Adult Should Strength Train. *Nautilus.* Summer

Wilmore, J., and Costill D. (1994) *Physiology of Sport and Exercise.* Human Kinetics Publishers, Champaign, Illinois.